THE
INTELLIGENT
CORPORATION

THE
INTELLIGENT
CORPORATION

Creating a Shared Network
for Information and Profit

RUTH STANAT

American Management Association

This book is available at a special
discount when ordered in bulk quantities.
For information, contact Special Sales Department,
AMACOM, a division of American Management Association,
135 West 50th Street, New York, NY 10020.

This publication is designed to provide accurate and authorita-
tive information in regard to the subject matter covered. It is sold
with the understanding that the publisher is not engaged in
rendering legal, accounting, or other professional service. If legal
advice or other expert assistance is required, the services of a
competent professional person should be sought.

Library of Congress Cataloging-in-Publication Data

Stanat, Ruth.
    The intelligent corporation : creating a shared network for
    information and profit / Ruth Stanat.
        p.   cm.
    ISBN 0-8144-5957-9
    1. Business intelligence.   I. Title.
HD38.7.S7   1990   89-81028
658.4'7—dc20   CIP

Printing number

10   9   8   7   6   5   4   3   2   1

This book is dedicated to
my three children,
Scott, Christine, and **Michael,** and my mother,
Ellen Corrigan, and my departed father,
James Francis Corrigan II.

Contents

Foreword

Global competition in local markets. Flexibility. Quality. Cost leadership. Product differentiation. Customer service. These are the watchwords of the 1990s which are leading to the evolution of the most dynamic, complex, and uncertain economic and business conditions of any decade in the twentieth century. No marketplace, industry, product, or service is exempted. Whether you are an executive in a firm that is or aspires to be in the Fortune 1000 or the INC. 100, the 1990s will make your head spin and create the worst case of information anxiety—the difference between usable information and information overload—known to modern executives.

To keep your information anxiety in check, you will require, and perhaps even demand, usable intelligence, information, and knowledge in easily digestible and timely doses in whatever printed or electronic form you believe is appropriate. Moreover, you may even expect that your portable or desktop PC will provide a window on the information network in your company that permits you to access the kernels of information and competitor intelligence residing in the company's R&D, product design, production, distribution, marketing, sales, and services activities. In addition, you will need to use that PC window to view external information on your competitors, your industry, and the local and global markets in which you do business.

To fulfill this tall order in the 1990s, strategic information management in business will mean taking seriously two important principles: (1) that the value of competitive and market intelligence is directly proportional to the complexity and uncertainty of domestic and global markets; and (2) that usable information, intelligence, and knowledge are directly proportional to the value executives and senior managers attach to their investments in information resources and technology.

Ruth Stanat's *The Intelligent Corporation* is a practical, how-to book which provides both the rationale and the methods for improving the strategic intelligence a business needs. She provides thoughtful and innovative approaches to discovering, packaging, digesting, and presenting usable business intelligence from international, market-oriented, and industry sources as well as methods for improving the internal value of a company's intelligence gathered from the sales and marketing work force. She observes that while many leading companies are beginning to recognize the value of usable business intelligence and organize to get it, the vast majority of businesses still undervalue and underestimate this critical resource. Perhaps for followers in any industry, not much can be done; however, for executives and managers who want their companies to prosper and not just to survive the 1990s, Ruth Stanat's concise, case-oriented guidance on building information-sharing networks and intelligence services that really work is a must read.

As president of her own strategic intelligence company which serves the Fortune 100 and as a former corporate executive involved in strategic planning, marketing, and product development, Ruth Stanat's timely knowledge and experience are reflected throughout this book. While most other books in this field emphasize either business information sources or techniques for acquiring strategic intelligence, *The Intelligent Corporation* really covers both topics and adds useful guidance on how to utilize information technology from PCs to modern communications networks to capture and add value to the competitive intelligence a business really needs.

Dr. Donald A. Marchand
Dean and Professor,
School of Information Studies
Syracuse University
Syracuse, New York

Acknowledgments

Without the contribution of key individuals and leaders of information technology from major U.S. corporations, this book would not have been possible. A list of information technology leaders of corporate America who contributed case studies and insight to *The Intelligent Corporation* follows:

Pat Arcadipane, Citibank
Tim Armour, Citibank
Laura Hunt, Digital Equipment Corporation
June Klein, Chase Manhattan Bank N.A.
Brenda Lewis, Transactions Marketing Inc.
Rick Linder, Ford Motor Company
Denise Lipkvitch, General Electric
Margo Magid, Citibank
Jim Onalfo, General Foods USA
Blair Peters, Kraft Foods, Inc.
Doug Phillips, Merck & Co., Inc.
Dr. Leon Schwartz, Pitney Bowes, Inc.
Joe Sonk, SquibbMark
Marty Stark, AT&T
Peggy Yocher, People's Bank

There are some key people who helped draft the book. Without the coauthoring of Ed Rubinstein, Project Director of Strategic Intelligence Systems, Inc., and his dedication to the editing process, this book would not exist. Also, I wish to thank Eva Weiss, AMACOM Developmental Editor, for her diligence to the content and editing of the book. In addition, my thanks to Judy Supersad, Supervisor of Administration for Strategic Intelligence Systems, Inc., for her electronic processing of many drafts of the book. Lastly, I wish to thank Dr. Donald Marchand, Dean of the School of Information Studies of Syracuse University, for writing the Foreword.

THE
INTELLIGENT
CORPORATION

1

Introduction to "Strategic Intelligence"

"The finest companies constantly seek to build their value on two dimensions: the value they provide to the customer, and the value they provide to their shareholders. These companies can differentiate among data, information, and intelligence, and have all three. Each is vital to building the bottom line."

Margo Magid, Director,
Strategic Planning Group, Citibank

In today's business environment, it goes without saying that information can make or break a company. Almost any business information may be termed "strategic intelligence," depending on how it is used. Oftentimes, the information includes valuable data on your competition's finances, manufacturing processes, products, or advertising and promotion budgets. Depending on various definitions, however, strategic intelligence can also involve areas like marketing research, strategic planning, legal affairs, field sales, and so on. We may therefore define strategic intelligence as the gathering, synthesis, and dissemination of strategic and tactical information in a systematic and timely manner for the purpose of developing a shared information network.

The shared information network, which is discussed in greater detail in Chapter 2, acts as a central depository of intelligence for an organization. As the word "network" implies, it also acts as a system of interconnected or cooperating individuals whose functions are to gather, analyze, and disseminate information for decision-making purposes.

1

All of us read newspapers, listen to the radio, watch television, and try to be as well-informed as we can, and yet, many are unaware of the major underlying trends in our country. Although corporations are wisely investing their resources in keeping abreast of new trends in their industries, now more than ever, environmental intelligence has become a key aspect of strategic intelligence. For instance, industries have had to react to a resurgence in environmental concerns and issues. The global warming trend, often referred to as the greenhouse effect, has broad-based implications for business and industry. A key contributor to this trend has been the use of a series of chemicals known as chlorofluorocarbons (CFCs). These chemicals are depleting the atmosphere's ozone layer, resulting in higher levels of harmful ultraviolet radiation that is being absorbed by the earth's surface and its inhabitants. Businesses and industries have had to make strategic decisions to respond to the greenhouse effect, by either banning the use of CFCs, conducting research to find alternatives for CFCs, or developing products that are environmentally safe.

Yet, in various corporate departments of many industries, professionals who are attempting to become information brokers within their organization very often find that they are buried with information and develop the dreaded case of information overload.

According to Margo Magid, director of the Strategic Planning Group at Citibank, "The financial services industry runs the risk of drowning in data: economic and financial facts, bits of customer and marketplace data, and episodic tracking of competitors' behavior. To overcome this hurdle," she says, "bits of business data must be integrated to create relevant business information. Technology has helped us by providing speed and analytic power. The scope and structure of these information systems, however, can create a new set of hurdles. Senior management can become dependent upon technicians and analysts to source and interpret vital business information, in effect isolating the decision maker from the 'real time' pulse of their business."

Finally, Magid asserts, "The strongest firms have transformed business information into intelligence. These firms have carried business information to business strategies. Their information systems reveal not only where they are, but what they can achieve going forward and how to do so cost-effectively. They can assess business performance relative to strategic goals, customer expectation, and competitive performance. The information at their fingertips is a synthesis of what they need to know to invest the next dollar most profitably, beat the competition to the punch, and anticipate customer needs."

The Evolution of Corporate Intelligence Systems

Many executives from both large and small companies are often intimidated by the term "intelligence systems." Most corporate executives feel a strong aversion to building large-scale systems that involve significant capital and human resources and that may prove to be of little value to the company. For this reason, it is far more effective to focus on building a program that offers high impact on bottom line results of the company.

The most successful programs are not initiated with the building of large-scale systems. They often start with a department or a person who has the charter for gathering and disseminating business or competitive intelligence, for example, marketing research, strategic planning, controllers, the information center, or an individual in an operating division.

Whatever the specifics of the job function, the individuals involved have to quickly develop a methodology for the ongoing scanning, synthesis, and dissemination of this information to various departments. In a small business, the marketing or sales department typically performs this function because it is closer to the customers in the field. In many large organizations, the marketing or sales department can actually "feed" information from field settings into a corporate intelligence system. This book provides a methodology for setting up a corporate intelligence system.

Changes in the Corporate Environment

At this early stage, it is helpful to gain a perspective on the changing nature of the marketing function, which has evolved substantially within corporations. In the past, the marketing function was considered the "nuts and bolts" of the organization. In addition to actually developing, pricing, distributing, and promoting products and services, marketing departments were the sole information centers of corporations.

With regard to the competitive environment, American industries were just beginning to emerge after World War II. That is, many industries were newly formed or re-formed industries created by technological innovations, emerging consumer needs, or other economic and sociological changes that elevated a new product or service to the level of a viable business opportunity. Clearly, the number of emerging industries has declined over the years. Consequently, the marketing function has changed drastically, altering the makeup of corporations and contributing to the so-called downsizing trend during the 1980s.

During the 1950s, the marketing research function flourished as consumer packaged goods companies and industrial companies continually defined the market needs of consumers and the manufacturing environment. Intelligence gathering took the form of "field surveys," focus groups, retail audits, and large-scale primary and syndicated secondary research projects.

This trend continued during the 1960s and became more sophisticated through the 1970s and into the 1980s with the influx of strategic planning departments. These departments applied sophisticated analytical techniques to environmental information, financial data, and marketing information. Consequently, the strategic planning function evolved into powerful departments in many large companies. The pitfalls of this function, however, were twofold:

1. The function was not an ongoing process. Large staffs of highly skilled analysts would gather and assemble information once or twice a year and produce a large document that outlined the five- or ten-year strategy along with specific objectives of the company. After the document was produced, the information became quickly outdated as the business environment kept changing.

2. It was difficult to tie the strategic plan to bottom line operating results. Although fancy three-ring binders were produced and distributed throughout the company, most of these documents stagnated and gathered dust on bookshelves.

Effects of These Changes in Strategic Planning

As strategic planning has evolved, so have other aspects of organizations. Three important changes are (1) the tendency toward downsizing, (2) the development of competitive intelligence operations, and (3) the increasing sophistication of information centers.

Downsizing

"Flattening" and downsizing have been common in recent years. One estimate has it that organizations have shed more than one million managers and staff professionals since 1979. As companies have reduced the number of middle managers, senior managers have increased their span of control and assumed additional responsibilities. Consider these two companies' stories.

New Information System for Top Management

Within weeks after a comprehensive restructuring thinned management by 40 percent, the president of a large oil company requested an improved management control system for his newly appointed senior management team. In response, a sophisticated, on-line executive information system was developed. It did the work of scores of analysts and midlevel managers whose responsibilities had been to produce charts and graphs, communicate this information, and coordinate operations with others in the company. The president also mandated the use of electronic mail to streamline communication throughout the business.

Integration Through Telecommunications

A large manufacturing company recently undertook a massive restructuring to cut the cost and time required to bring a new product to market. The effort included layoffs, divestitures, and early retirements, which thinned middle management by 30 percent. The company adopted a sophisticated telecommunications network, which linked all parts of the multinational company, and a centralized corporate data base, which integrated all aspects of the highly decentralized business. Senior managers used the data base and networks to summarize and display data from inside and outside the company and to signal to employees the kinds of things they should focus on.[1]

A key element that can be gleaned from these two examples is that information and the technologies that have evolved from information management, which have historically been considered tools for organizational expansion, have become tools for downsizing and restructuring. In addition, organizations are creating new information channels that are effectively centralizing decision making. These elements have further increased the need to effectively manage the information flow within organizations.

Competitive Intelligence

With the structural changes of U.S. corporations and the intensely competitive dynamics that have become preva-

---

[1] These two stories are reprinted by permission of the *Harvard Business Review*. Excerpt from "Information Technology and Tomorrow's Manager" by Lynda M. Applegate, James I. Cash, Jr., and D. Quinn Mills (November–December 1988). Copyright © 1988 by the President and Fellows of Harvard College; all rights reserved.

lent, top management feels the need, and rightly so, to shape their strategy in part according to the activities of their competitors. In fact, many U.S. industries have become so competitive that the only way for a company to win new customers is to "steal" them from its competitors. This is the impetus for competitive intelligence and the systematic monitoring of the competition.

Nowadays, more and more companies are systematically tracking their competitors. A 1988 study commissioned by the Conference Board, a well-known and respected research organization, surveyed top and middle management from 315 companies in a wide variety of industries. Fifty-nine percent of top management and 68 percent of middle managers surveyed considered monitoring the competition "very important."

There are various forms of competitive information or intelligence that are valuable in today's environment. To many companies, the most valuable competitive information deals with strategy, pricing, and sales. The most valuable sources of competitive intelligence are the following:

- The sales force of an organization
- The customers of an organization
- Published information from trade/industry periodicals, newspapers, magazines

During the 1980s, a key objective of many organizations was to develop a systematic approach to implementing a competitive tracking program. Many of the organizations, however, found that integrating competitive information with other vital information sources was difficult.

Corporate Information Centers

To meet the need for gathering various types of intelligence, "information centers" also proliferated in corporations in the 1980s. Their initial intent was to apply technology to data gathering to support the reduced staff departments (strategic planning, market research, business development, controllers, research and development). In some cases, companies made significant investments in these centers and spent thousands of dollars in hardware and software technology, with little regard for the content or the focus of the information. In other cases, traditional corporate libraries came to be called information centers as personal computing became second nature.

To add emphasis to the information center, electronic data base publishers began to market textual data bases offering information on just about every topic imaginable. To support use of these hundreds and even thousands of data bases, data base distributors began to develop sophisticated, yet "user friendly" software packages for users to navigate the data base maze to find the desired piece of information. As a result, corporate planners and researchers, just having learned to turn on the personal computer, now found they had to obtain another business degree in electronic data base technology!

Some of these corporate information centers have been more successful than others, and some companies have even realized a return on their investments. Information centers that have implemented technology, when it made sense to do so, have experienced the most success. Additionally, those information centers staffed with research and business professionals have experienced credibility and success with users from the operating divisions. These information centers act as intelligence centers.

General Electric: Success Story—
Evolution From Information Center to Intelligence Center

A multibillion-dollar corporation formed a corporate marketing information center following the paring down of large strategic planning and marketing staffs. The initial mission of the information center was to provide marketing and planning staffs in the operating divisions with information regarding their corporate accounts through a quick turnaround service. During the mid-1980s, the information center was centralized and employed two or three professionals who had extensive electronic data base expertise. The information center was actively used for quick-access information requests. The division personnel, however, were searching for more than raw information. They were searching for analysis.

To meet this need, the corporate marketing information center developed value-added, packaged analytical reports that included competitor and customer account profiles. These reports were custom-designed for division executives to enable them to obtain a "snapshot" of their customers and their competitors. In spite of the success of these reports, the divisions were still searching for the next step—the ongoing tracking of key events in their lines of business.

To keep abreast of these key events, the information center is evaluating development of customized data bases that track and analyze key events within the industry and customer business segments. This evolution will enable the information center to evolve into a profit center and track the effectiveness of the service and products provided to the operating divisions. The net result is that this information center has become an intelligence center that provides actionable information—that is, it helps the decision makers.[2]

A Survey on Information Needs: How Does Your Company Stack Up?

A survey conducted over the past five years by Strategic Intelligence Systems, Inc. examines the information networking needs of a majority of the Fortune 100 firms. Specifically, the survey analyzes responses from phone calls, formal and informal interviews, and actual audits or "needs analysis" projects. The survey was unstructured at times. The exact questions, however, remained constant and the departments varied from firm to firm. The results of the

---

[2]Used with permission of General Electric.

survey were derived from the responses of mid- to senior-level executives from the following departments:

- Strategic planning
- Marketing research
- Product development
- Financial planning
- Corporate information center
- Corporate library

All respondents answered the following questions:

- What department within your firm is responsible for competitive intelligence gathering or functions as a centralized repository for information?
- Do you have a formalized process for the systematic gathering of intelligence on a routine basis and a mechanism for distributing or accessing the information?
- What is your annual budget for this type of information, including staff resources, salaries, purchase of outside information sources, purchase of international information?
- What do you spend on outside consulting services?
- What happens to internally generated documents within your organization?
- What are your current and future information needs?
- How frequently do you need this type of information?
- In what format do you need the information?

Results of the Survey

The following sections outline the survey results through the first half of 1988. For perspective, data are included from 1985 to show the growth of business intelligence networks. The data illustrate that large organizations have realized the need for an information center, which has become a centralized repository for information and the lifeline of these organizations. The data in Table 1-1 signify the "enlightenment" of management over the past five years toward this concept. The table shows that a centralized intelligence network was not considered an integral part of

Table 1-1. Information needs survey of Fortune 100 firms, 1985 versus 1988.

Function	1985	1988
Has a centralized repository for capturing and storing information	25%	60%
Has a systematic method for scanning and analyzing information on a daily or weekly basis	10%	40%
Has an electronic system to process this information	10%	40%
Has a mechanism to store and provide access to internal documents	5%	40%
Has initiated a strategic information audit that quantifies the firm's investment in internal and external information and defines information needs	10%	35%
Is a low/medium/high priority	low	medium–high
Departmental responsibility	Marketing/Planning Executive staff Corporate librarians International divisions	Marketing/Planning

Source: Strategic Intelligence Systems, Inc., 1989.

(continued)

Table 1-1. (continued)

Function	1985	1988
Annual budget expenditure, including department salaries, purchased outside information sources, software and computer charges, and consultants ($000)	$150–$250	$500–$750
Internal staff	2–3	4–6
System has become part of the decision-making process of the organization	low–minimal	moderate–high
Impact of the system or department	too low to quantify results	moderate (just beginning)

most major firms as late as 1985. As corporate staffs have thinned out during the past three to four years, more firms have recognized the need for such a network. Of significance is the growth of electronic systems to 40 percent of the Fortune 100 firms.

Segmentation by Sophistication of Information Network

What if your company is a Fortune 50, 100, 500, or 1,000 firm? Data show a direct correlation between size of firm and degree of sophistication of the information-gathering function (see Table 1-2).

From Table 1-2, we can generalize that the larger the firm, the stronger the need for systematically capturing internal and external information. In addition, the more decentralized the decision-making responsibility, the greater the need for these information networks.

Table 1-2. Segmentation of Fortune 50–1,000 firms.

Function	Fortune 50	Fortune 100	Fortune 500	Fortune 1,000
Has a centralized repository	85%	60%	40%	20%
Has an electronic system	60%	40%	25%	5%
Has developed customized corporate intelligence data bases	60%	35%	20%	<5%
Uses hard copy	65%	70%	85%	95%
Annual budget expenditure ($000)	$750–$1,000+	$500–$750	$250–$500	$0–$250
Staff commitment	6–8+	4–6	2–4	0–2
Profit center	yes	yes	no	no

Source: Strategic Intelligence Systems, Inc., 1989.

Mix of Information Vehicles

Despite the wide range of formalized networks, intelligence gathering exists in various formats. As such, organizations that provide these services for corporations have increased the depth and breadth of intelligence. This expansion parallels the trend toward providing value-added products and services. Corporate executives are demanding products that analyze and synthesize data and textual information. In addition, these executives are also demanding consulting and training services that assess their information resources and needs. Table 1-3 shows the products and services offered by business intelligence networks or centers.

The table indicates that Fortune 50 firms appear to be more "proactive" in providing information for planning, whereas Fortune 1,000 firms tend to be more "reactive" to quick information requests resulting from specific events in the marketplace.

Table 1-3.   Information product mix, 1988.

Type of Information	Fortune 50 (%)	Fortune 100 (%)	Fortune 500 (%)	Fortune 1,000 (%)
Full-scale analytical projects and data bases	60	40	25	<15
Ad hoc research reports	20	30	30	20
Quick information requests	10	20	40	60
Consulting and training	10	10	5	<5
Total	100	100	100	≈100

Source: Strategic Intelligence Systems, Inc., 1989.

Domestic Versus International Information

Many multinational firms have stretched their territorial domains and view the globe as their marketplace. In addition, with the planned elimination of European Common Market trade barriers in 1992, more organizations are looking to integrate international information. Table 1-4 illustrates that large, multinational companies are actively integrating international intelligence into their information networks.

Table 1-4 also underscores increased foreign competition in our markets, particularly affecting multinational firms that are based in the United States. It also demonstrates the strategic thrust of U.S.-based corporations to compete more effectively on a global scale and to actively pursue and expand into new markets.

Timeliness of Information

In today's fast-paced business environment, information is being generated at speeds that would break the sound

Table 1-4.   Domestic versus international information.

	Scope of Information Needs	
	Domestic (%)	International (%)
Fortune 50 Firms		
1985	80	20
1988	65	35
Fortune 100 Firms		
1985	85	15
1988	70	30
Fortune 500/1,000 Firms		
1985	90	10
1988	85	15

Source: Strategic Intelligence Systems, Inc., 1989.

barrier, and organizations are demanding intelligence as fast as it is generated. This timeliness factor is illustrated in Table 1-5, which also shows that smaller firms require more timely information than the larger firms.

The "Intelligence Scale": Phases in the Development of a Business Intelligence Network

The following four phases are involved in developing an intelligence network. They can serve as a benchmark for organizations implementing a network and are especially useful for those "stuck" at a certain phase.

Phase I: Corporate Awareness

In this phase, the company does not have a formalized process for gathering and synthesizing external information from published sources. Additionally, the company does not maintain an internal library of source documents that are distributed within the organization. Typically, these documents are in the form of interoffice memos, competi-

Table 1-5. Timeliness of information.

	Frequency of Information Needs		
	Quarterly (%)	Monthly (%)	Daily (%)
Fortune 50/100 Firms			
1985	40	40	20
1988	30	30	40
Fortune 500/1,000 Firms			
1985	30	30	40
1988	25	25	50

Source: Strategic Intelligence Systems, Inc., 1989.

tive information obtained from sales representatives, and internally published studies on a particular market or competitor. The organization does recognize the need for developing a shared information network that is derived from internal and external sources. In addition, a strategic information audit is conducted during the corporate awareness phase. (Chapter 4 contains a discussion of the development of a strategic information audit and an actual case.)

Depending on various factors, such as the culture of the organization, its mission, and its current business position, corporate awareness may be difficult to develop. Gaining awareness and acceptance of the need for an intelligence network may depend on the efforts of an "internal champion" or department to make management aware of the need for such a network. (An "internal champion" simply refers to someone who develops awareness and initiates the process of developing an intelligence network.)

Phase II: Establishment of a Department or Process to Gather Information

In this phase, the organization identifies a department or group of people (or functional area) responsible for gathering internal and external intelligence. Principally, the department's activities are as follows:

- Formation of a centralized corporate library
- Distribution of hard copy daily clippings from published sources
- Distribution of a newsletter
- Sporadic generation of reports that profile or analyze the competitors of the organization
- Occasional use of external information providers
- Heavy use of external consultants on a per project basis

In most of today's corporations, the actual department most closely associated with these activities is the corporate library or information center. During this phase, the library

or information center establishes a process for gathering
internal and external intelligence sources. Although these
departments have become vital settings in most corporations, the intelligence-gathering effort has become prevalent
across various business units and divisions of an organization.

With the shrinking size of internal staffs, the intelligence-gathering process is usually augmented by contracting with external research firms that specialize in developing intelligence procedures. Nowadays, many of these firms
have become valuable resources to organizations during this
phase.

The most formidable task during this phase is to integrate internal and external information sources in a manner
that is cost-effective, easily accessible to management, and
most important, actionable. Internal and external intelligence sources are discussed in detail in Chapters 5 and 6,
respectively.

Phase III: Development of an Electronic System

Now that the organization has developed a process for
gathering intelligence and information sharing is a major
objective, the next step is to develop a business or corporate
intelligence network that combines critical internal documents and captures external information on a systematic
basis. During this phase, the company outlines the information architecture or the actual blueprint of the intelligence network.

Because the objective of the network is to have intelligence available throughout the organization, the network
involves multiple user departments and generally has a
complex information architecture. Chapter 2, "The Shared
Information Network," discusses information architecture
in greater detail, cites several examples of this process
within corporations, and discusses the integral components
for an electronic shared information network.

In this phase, the company actually has an operational
system with select users. The system will continue to evolve
until it reaches Phase IV.

Phase IV: Development of a Global Electronic Network

In this phase, all functional departments are actively using the system, which has evolved into a global electronic intelligence network. The following list outlines what such a global electronic network can accomplish and the inputs and outputs of such a system:

- An electronic system with more than one hundred users on the system from all functional departments and divisions
- A system that is proactive and provides relevant and timely intelligence to the end user
- A systematic method for scanning and synthesizing information on a daily, monthly, or quarterly basis, according to the specific needs of corporate staff and the operating divisions
- A method for putting critical internal documents into the system
- A method for capturing field sales and manufacturing intelligence and incorporating this information into the system
- A method for capturing international information on a timely basis
- A source of several information products for corporate executives (data base access, newsletters, quarterly reports)
- A mechanism for periodic review of the system and process that constantly evolves to meet changing business conditions
- A cost-efficient system that reduces duplication of effort between departments and between external information suppliers and consultants
- A system that becomes part of the planning process and serves as critical input for decision making

Given these four phases, one might ask: How many firms are at each phase? From the data obtained from the Fortune 1,000 survey discussed earlier, we can estimate the distribution (see Figure 1-1).

Figure 1-1. Percentage distribution of firms by development phase, 1989.

Phase I	Phase II	Phase III	Phase IV
Timeframe for development: 6 months – 1 year	Timeframe for development: 1 – 2 years	Timeframe for development: 6 months – 2 years	Timeframe for development: Ongoing
90% of the Fortune 50 60% of the Fortune 100 50% of the Fortune 500 25% of the Fortune 1,000	80% of the Fortune 50 50% of the Fortune 100 40% of the Fortune 500 20% of the Fortune 1,000	60% of the Fortune 50 40% of the Fortune 100 30% of the Fortune 500 10% of the Fortune 1,000	40% of the Fortune 50 30% of the Fortune 100 20% of the Fortune 500 >5% of the Fortune 1,000

Source: Strategic Intelligence Corporation, Inc., 1989.

Figure 1-1 indicates that most U.S. corporations have not fully developed their intelligence networks. The actual cases presented in this book provide clear examples of corporations that have taken the initial steps toward building a corporate intelligence network. Although all the corporations discussed have approached their intelligence network in a different manner, the results parallel the ultimate goal of Phase IV.

Strategic intelligence systems or networks are not easy to implement. They involve top–down commitment from senior-level management, in addition to extensive coordination from several functional departments—planning, marketing, information systems, controllers, and the operating divisions. The culture or the politics of an organization can be either an asset or a liability to the execution of these systems. In general, companies that are highly centralized experience a greater degree of success with a top–down approach, and decentralized companies exhibit a higher degree of success with a bottom–up approach. Examples of these approaches are discussed in Chapter 4.

The concept of a corporate intelligence system or a shared information network also goes against the traditional practice of "information hoarding" within corporations. Additionally, these systems involve "turf" problems. Executives often ask the question, Where should I reside? More important, some traditional staff departments are threatened by the electronic dissemination of information that was traditionally generated in hard copy from their departments. On the other hand, some of these systems have been known to dissolve barriers of communication between specific departments. These issues cannot be ignored because it takes people and a team effort to make the systems work.

How does the group responsible for developing such a network or the internal champion overcome the issue of politics? The strategic information audit and a methodology to ensure "buy in" from diverse groups within the organization are discussed in Chapter 4. Although politics exist in every organization, these networks have been successfully implemented in many companies. Even with the potential obstacles, the group or internal champion can proceed cautiously with the execution of the system.

Strategic Intelligence—So What's New?

During the past two years, many information and intelligence gatherers have claimed that they give corporations the highly sought-after "competitive edge." Despite all this marketing lingo, there are certain building blocks that will enable an organization to achieve an advantage through intelligence and the design of a system that enables managers to stay current in the marketplace. As we enter the next century, networks that integrate strategic and tactical intelligence will be the nerve centers of leading businesses.

In establishing such networks, corporations must first examine their strategic objectives and their internal and external information sources to ensure customized intelligence systems or data bases. These systems should be installed prior to the application of the next wave of technology—artificial intelligence. This foundation must first be laid because large organizations are typically slow to change. It is clear that an infrastructure must be built that can support the organization.

The Goal: A Corporate Intelligence Network

"Corporate intelligence network" sounds like a very fancy and upscale title that only the Fortune 50 firms could afford. Every company, however, regardless of the size or complexity of organization, has a need to develop a process for its information gathering and dissemination. Smaller firms, in particular, have a need for a process to track their business environment, their competition, their markets, their field sales activity, and new developments in technology. For these firms, an intelligence network, no matter how simple in design, can be the key to survival.

For larger firms with multiple functions and departments, a strategic intelligence network is necessary to increase the efficiency within the organization and to keep management abreast of the global and domestic competitive environments. Actual cases discussed in later chapters take you through the way both large and small firms have developed such a process and how they use it to their advantage.

The chapters that follow identify significant issues that must be addressed and, ultimately, acted upon. Cases are included that outline successes and failures relevant to those issues. As you read through each chapter, ask yourself the following questions:

How well do we fare in this process?
Do we have a process to address this issue?
Are we staffed adequately to implement this process?
Do we have the appropriate information content?
How efficient is the investment we have made in hardware and software in relation to the end goal, development of a corporate intelligence network?

Regardless of the size of your business, strategic intelligence has a powerful impact on the future of your business. Several companies have awakened to this concept and have taken action to build their network. As you read through the book, use each of the chapters as a benchmark to gauge your efforts. Those companies that do not initiate a corporate intelligence network might find themselves either paralyzed by information overload or noncompetitive because of lack of appropriate information. Those with such a network will become the intelligent corporations of the twenty-first century.

This book is intended to answer the question, How does an organization develop a business intelligence network? For many corporations, such networks (1) result in significant cost savings, (2) provide decision support capabilities, and (3) allow the company to become more competitive in today's highly competitive business environment. The book contains numerous cases from both identified and unidentified Fortune 100 firms that have implemented a shared information network, reorganized methods of gathering and disseminating information, and already reaped the benefits of such a network. If you are actively involved in developing a shared information network, you may wish to compare the efforts of your organization with those of the companies presented here. To assist you, Chapter 3 includes a step-by-step approach to develop a network, including a work plan to provide a critical conceptual time frame for the development.

Summary

There are many factors influencing the need for expanded, timely business intelligence networks—among them, corporate downsizing, decentralization, and global thrust. The fact is that organizations with fully developed information networks will have an important advantage over their competitors during the 1990s and beyond.

2

The Shared
Information Network

"The client need is very clear and urgent. They want relevant, timely, and cost-efficient answers to their questions. Information service units must organize to respond to these needs. In our case, this meant creating a new information center dedicated to managing and disseminating primary, syndicated, and public information with a business mentality."

Blair Peters, Group Research Manager,
Kraft Foods, Inc.

How many times have you been in a meeting or in a discussion with your boss and tried to remember an article you read on a key competitor or event within your industry or marketplace? You may have clipped the article, filed it in a folder, or just made a mental note of its content. You need supporting documentation, however, to make your point. What do you do?

At the bare minimum, it is necessary for you to locate the magazine, find the article, reread the article, and perhaps find other articles to support your case. Similarly, within your organization someone may have published a study on a certain topic and may have subsequently left the company. You will quickly realize that when the author of the report leaves the company, so does the author's intelligence. You are now faced with the task of retrieving information generated internally within the organization in addition to staying abreast of all the information published by sources external to your company. How can a human being absorb and digest all this information and still do an effective job?

Organizations need a way to obtain information that affects their business and are searching for an effective mechanism that will enable them to integrate their internal intelligence networks with vital external information. They need a shared information network.

In developing such a network, an organization must follow a series of steps, which are detailed in Chapter 3. These steps can prove difficult to implement, however, because of various issues. In this chapter we examine the issues involved in developing a corporate intelligence network to provide a framework for such a network and to avoid stumbling blocks to implementing the steps discussed in Chapter 3.

The Basic Issue

Let's take the case of the small business. The president of the company has perhaps a handful of people who represent his or her management team. The information flows freely on a daily basis in this "flat" organization. If someone in this small company picks up the paper and notices a new promotional program initiated by a competitor and posts the ad on the bulletin board, nearly everyone in the firm is notified of the event by midmorning. As a company grows in size and as layers of management are added, achieving this "instant competitive intelligence" becomes more and more of a task. This problem is exemplified by a company with multiple field locations, both domestic and abroad. In short, large and midsize corporations are faced with the challenge of achieving the goal of rapid access to intelligence.

Why Share Information?

Most organizations experience the "hoarding of intelligence." No matter what size the company, corporate executives have begun to realize that information is power. Nowadays, as the size of organizations fluctuates, less and less information is documented or catalogued. Yet, the hoarding of information is inherent to the management system in both large and small companies because managers are rewarded for innovative ideas and original thinking.

The hoarding of intelligence is exacerbated with increased size and complexity of an organization. Large corporations that are decentralized and have numerous operating divisions are faced with a tremendous amount of duplication of effort. In one company, more than six different departments generate studies on the same topic area at the same time. How many times have you just finished looking up some information to discover that a report in another department already contains the information? This hoarding of intelligence puts companies at a competitive disadvantage. Companies that can quickly retrieve internal information and efficiently synthesize and disseminate external information have an advantage over those organizations that cannot. Furthermore, each manager or executive is a data base of information, with years of functional and industry expertise making him a resident expert on certain topics. Getting access to your coworkers' or subordinates' areas of expertise requires that you tap into their data bank of information, which is stored in their brain. Thus, the "infoglut" factor has led to the increased emphasis on and importance of information sharing within organizations. Consider this actual story:

Reducing the Information Glut

A major consumer products firm prided itself on the dissemination of marketing information on a worldwide basis. Much of the internal documentation, however, included forty-page memos that summarized worldwide marketing meetings. Additionally, more than one hundred staff members were copied on these memos worldwide. Calculations showed that at least two months of an administrator's time were required just to copy and disseminate this correspondence. In this case, it was recommended that the firm condense this semiannual paper into a two- to three-page summary and put the document into their electronic mail package, which could be accessed by all their affiliates in the United States and abroad. This system significantly reduced the duplication of effort within the organization, thus reducing their infoglut factor.

Thus, an effective shared information network can work to resolve infoglut and information hoarding, two factors that can negatively affect the efficiency with which organizations manage the universe of information. When companies recognize the need for a shared information network, they are faced with the following issues:

- What is system architecture, and what components of this make up a shared information network?
- Who or what functional area is responsible for gathering, selecting, and disseminating information?
- What type of information should be "shared"?
- What format can be used to distribute the information, and what should it look like?
- How is this type of information effectively distributed?
- What resource requirements are necessary to effectively implement this process?
- How does the company measure the effectiveness of the process?
- What are the pitfalls of these programs?

The following sections address each of these issues.

System Architecture

From a broad perspective, "system architecture" can be defined as the *visual representation of a system through which information provided by source documents is changed into final documents.* Clearly, the purpose of systematizing information is to maintain the basic elements of input–process–output. This allows an organization with a large infrastructure to sustain itself. In my experience, I have found no single system architecture appropriate for the development of a shared information network. The flow and circulation of information is largely based on the structure of the organization, as well as the corporate culture. Figure 2-1 depicts a simple system architecture in which a data base and other forms of information are derived from source documents.

In this simple example, internal and external information sources are pulled together to create a data base. Such a data base, which increases in value over time, can become part of a corporatewide intelligence network and the center for distribution of information in various forms (for example, company newsletters and quarterly reports).

Consider the history of system architecture. During the 1950s and 1960s, the concept of system architecture was confined to accounting or transactions systems. Such systems were data processing systems run on behalf of accountants. Transactions systems, which were used by various professionals, not just accountants, began to evolve in the late 1960s and early 1970s. Their distinguishing characteristic: They capture data as the transaction occurs, in "real time"—not after the fact—through a variety of input meth-

Figure 2-1. A simple system architecture.

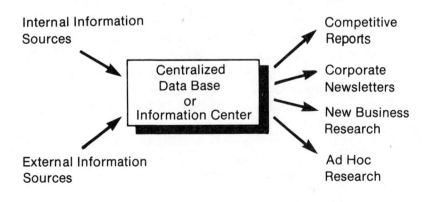

Internal Information Sources

External Information Sources

Centralized Data Base or Information Center

Competitive Reports

Corporate Newsletters

New Business Research

Ad Hoc Research

ods including scanning, user entry on-line, and electronic coding (credit cards). *Data* are transformed upon entry into readily accessible, usable *information* by the sophisticated software used in these systems. Thus, in their most evolved form, these systems are called "strategic information systems": The transaction information is shared with the customer, supplier, or distributor of the product or service, creating competitive advantage for each with timely, accurate information. For instance, strategic planners and market research professionals can now access textual and analytical information that provides them with timely information on their competitive environment.

According to Brenda Lewis, president of Transactions Marketing Inc., "The economic upheavals of the mid-1970s—quadrupled energy prices, deregulation of financial markets, advances in global communications and transportation, the rise of foreign competition as the dollar inflated—fostered dramatic changes in the need for competitive intelligence. Fortunately, the advent of the personal computer broke the accounting function's hammerlock on corporate data processing systems, with their emphasis on past performance data, and permitted the development of proactive marketing information systems, including competitive intelligence."

Today, the amount of information in textual form continues to increase. As a result, some organizations have become buried in information. Executives are searching for effective ways to capture, store, disseminate, and most important, share timely information that is relevant to their business; in other words, they are seeking a systematized shared information network. When applied to a shared information network, "system architecture" refers to the following components:

- The "flow" of information
- The technology-based components involved in developing these systems
- The end-user community

Information Flow

Within an organization, "information flow" refers to any number of formal or informal processes that circulate information. In many organizations, this flow can be very simple and involve numerous forms. It may involve such informal processes as information obtained from telephone conversations, distribution of interoffice or routing memos, and internally published newsletters and bulletins. Thus, much of this information involves voice and hard copy. Information flow can also be quite sophisticated. Clearly, the larger and more diversified an organization is, the more sophisticated is its information flow.

Typically, the information coordinators and corporate library gather mounds of information from the external environment (for instance, published sources) and from the operating divisions of the organization (for example, field sales information). In addition, they gather, filter, and disseminate competitive and strategic information and distribute key findings to top-level decision makers, in most cases senior executives.

A data base is a vehicle to store either textual or numeric information. Most of the information used in middle- to senior-level decision making is from textual sources (newspapers, periodicals, internal analyses, and reports). A data base, however, does not have to be a sophisticated computerized system. It can simply be a file folder of papers on your desk. The file folder, however, is organized according to a specific purpose and may contain papers on financial performance of a product line or competitive ads on your business. In short, you would go to look for specific information on a certain topic within a specific folder.

A growing amount of information is in textual form, not just numeric. The development of a system architecture involves putting both textual and numeric information into computers and making the information accessible through software programs. This has prompted many software publishers to develop sophisticated packages for computers that are designed to integrate market and financial data for the business analyst. Some software packages are marketed as the solution to all information needs (transaction processing, data analysis, graphics, and data management). As a result, new software products such as data base management systems and executive information systems often emerge.

The Technology

The technological components of a shared information network may be as simple as a single computer or workstation. Such a system works best when one person or a few people are responsible for accessing information that is then distributed as hard copy on an ad hoc basis or as requested by management. Thus, the technological components are very centralized and may serve the needs of a division or functional department of an organization. At the other extreme, the components may comprise a sophisticated electronic system in which information is continually accessed by many users throughout an organization. Some firms maintain large-scale information networks that utilize mainframe computers as well as sophisticated programming languages.

The application of technology and its architectural integration into intelligence networks will increase in the future. According to Jim Onalfo, systems manager for the desserts division of General Foods, "Companies in the nineties are going to survive because the executives in those companies know how to employ high-tech technology to improve their infrastructure. Those that do not have executives with these skills will fail and their companies will suffer."

For the development of a shared information network, the technological components are constantly evolving as advancements in information management are made. Artificial intelligence or expert systems are now performing functions usually associated with human intelligence, including reasoning, learning, and self-improvement. However, corporations must first develop their own internal intelligence network prior to the successful application of artificial intelligence systems. By the year 2000, those corporations that have successfully developed a corporate intelligence network probably will be able to apply artificial intelligence to the system architecture. In essence, these will be "intelligent data bases" able to emulate human intelligence to make projections into the future.

This communications component of system architecture provides a means to tie together a corporate intelligence network. As with hardware and software, a communications network may employ a high level of technology, for example an interactive information system such as a local area network or an electronic mail system. A sophisticated intelligence network usually involves the use of telecommunication devices (telephones, modems, PBXs, and so forth).

The technological components of a shared information network can be the driving force behind the network. Prior to the 1980s, all information was gathered and distributed manually and there did not exist a means to "pull it all together." Since the advent of the personal computer in the early 1980s, technology has affected how information is stored, distributed, updated, and archived. Clearly, the technological components of a shared information network vary with the information needs of an organization, its size, and its business and competitive environments. They also determine the effectiveness of a shared information network.

End-User Community

Probably the most important aspect of the system architecture of a network is its end-user community, because the end users of a network are responsible for turning information into intelligence. In addition to acting as the "voice" of the network, the end users must provide feedback about the network. Such feedback provides a necessary interactive and human element to the network and a "loop" to the overall system architecture. Thus, the architecture of the network will incorporate intelligence from such areas as field sales. Field sales intelligence systems are discussed in detail in Chapter 8.

It is necessary to keep in mind five key points about the system architecture of a shared information network:

1. Corporate intelligence networks do not have a single system architecture. They are based on the structure of an organization and its corporate culture.
2. Because a corporate intelligence network is designed to be efficient, the architecture exploits state-of-the-art technology.
3. The system architecture of the network has a continual feedback process and is constantly evolving and changing with the needs of the organization. Thus, the system must be interactive and involve people.
4. The system architecture is not volume-driven. The network should not become a source for archival information or information that is outdated. Rather, it should be a source for timely, high-value information that could affect the organization.
5. As more and more organizations expand their international presence, the architecture of a corporate intelligence network should be global in scope.

Responsibility for Developing the Intelligence Network

In many instances, one department may assume responsibility for developing the network to minimize duplication of effort and maximize productivity of information dissemination.

Unfortunately, there is no clear-cut guideline as to what department or functional area should be responsible for this task. Clearly, the organization of the company will dictate which departments are well-positioned to execute the network. The decision involved in delegating this responsibility can be based on various factors. Among them are the actual size of the organization, whether the organization is centralized or decentralized, the actual job responsibilities or job descriptions of each functional department within the organization, the type of information that the intelligence network will provide, and the strategic objectives of the network.

In most companies, corporate staff departments from the following functional areas have the capabilities to develop the network:

- Corporate/division marketing
- Information systems
- Strategic planning
- Corporate library

Corporate/Division Marketing

To meet the internal information needs of corporations, corporate marketing or strategic intelligence centers have been formed. In the past, this function was met by the traditional corporate library. However, as strategic planning and the concept of strategic marketing received greater emphasis from senior management, the corporate marketing departments became the most viable setting for a corporate intelligence network.

In today's business environment, many organizations have organized a corporate marketing information center. Compared with many other functions within an organization, marketing departments are most closely associated with the success or failure of the company's products or services. Thus, the development of an information center within the marketing department has become one of the most viable ways of gathering market and competitive information that is timely, accurate, and actionable.

As part of a centralized corporate intelligence network, the marketing department performs the functions of data gathering and data screening and analysis. That is, the department gathers information that is relevant to the organization's scope of business and disregards information that is not. Oftentimes, the department may even have its own in-house news clipping service or hire an external source for this chore.

When the corporate marketing function develops an intelligence network, the network acts as a support unit for the entire organization. It provides the organization with information from a wide variety of published sources (for instance, industry trade publications) and from other information providers (such as on-line commercial data bases). In addition, it honors quick-information requests from other functional areas of the organization. On a smaller scale, when the marketing department of a division or business unit develops an intelligence network, it acts as a test site or model for other departments of the organization to emulate.

Of course, there can be problems when a marketing division sets up an intelligence network. Although some marketing divisions take on a very proactive role, others are more reactive and do not respond favorably. Or, there may be a split among sections within the division. I developed a corporate intelligence network for one of the marketing divisions of a large packaged-food company. The division was organized into groups by type of product (for example, frozen, dry, or refrigerated). Because some of these groups were more successful than others, the responses to the idea of an intelligence network varied among the groups. The key to resolving this problem was to identify an internal champion who could help convince the negative factions that the network would be advantageous.

The members of marketing departments at the divisional level should realize the benefits they can reap from a shared intelligence network. They are much closer to the sales function than the members of other departments are, at both the divisional and corporate levels. By being so close to the sales force, the marketing department of a division can use the salespeople as an information source and use the intelligence network to keep the salespeople abreast of competitive, business, and environmental activity that may affect their role within the organization. The topic of field sales intelligence systems is discussed in Chapter 8.

Information Systems

By 1990, the information services sector is expected to account for 6 percent of the nation's gross national product. This estimate, combined with continued advances in technology, has led to the development of information systems (IS) departments in many corporations. A growing number of IS departments have actively become involved in developing corporate intelligence networks, especially because many have become more closely associated with the sales and marketing functions of organizations. In addition, the IS departments as a whole are increasing in manpower, corporate backing, and budgets to finance a shared information network. At the divisional level, also, IS departments usually respond very favorably to corporate intelligence networks.

The overall role of IS professionals will become much clearer in the future with regard to the corporate intelligence network. With the newly created title "chief information officer" (CIO) in many organizations, the IS function will gain a stronger presence in the corporate intelligence network, primarily because most CIOs have information systems or data processing backgrounds.

Strategic Planning

As the word "strategic" began to infiltrate corporations during the 1960s and 1970s, so too did strategic planning departments. Because "strategic" underscores the notion of competitive, business, and environmental intelligence for many organizations, the strategic planning department has become an information center and the basis for a corporate intelligence network in some organizations.

Within a corporate intelligence network, strategic planning departments serve some of the same functions as the corporate marketing department. Recognizing this duplication of effort, senior management in some corporations has centralized the corporate intelligence network in one department. This has become one of the major upheavals leading to the corporate downsizing trend that is now so prevalent. As a result, strategic planning departments are much smaller now than they were in the past.

Because of this downsizing, the strategic planning function often relies more heavily on external firms for research. In addition to developing intelligence networks, these departments request ad hoc research and analysis on such topics as internal business matters and competitor profiles. Whether the research is supplied on a one-shot or an ongoing basis, the key to this type of research is that it is future oriented. That is, the information is to be used as a planning tool and distributed to senior management.

Although the strategic planning department may not be the centralized setting for a corporate intelligence network, it does play a vital role in the evolution of the network. The strategic planning role can be part of a coordinated effort with other functions to develop an intelligence network.

Corporate Library

In many organizations, a corporate library provides the same type of services that public libraries provide for the general public. The corporate library is usually the department senior executives turn to when they need published information on an ad hoc basis. Yet, in some instances the corporate library acts as the functional area responsible for a corporate intelligence network. Corporate libraries are effective information centers for organizations and more and more are becoming the centralized setting for a corporate intelligence network.

As have most other functions within corporations, the corporate library has been negatively affected by the downsizing trend. Many corporate libraries have one or two persons with library science backgrounds who are solely responsible for maintaining a library, retrieving information requests, and keeping senior management abreast of competitive, business, and environmental events that affect the organization. In addition to these vital tasks, corporate librarians may play a very proactive role in the development of a corporate intelligence network.

Sometimes, it may take a coordinated effort between the corporate library department and another function to develop a corporate intelligence network, as in the following example.

Interdepartmental Intelligence Network

For a major consumer products/technology firm, developing a corporate intelligence network entailed pooling resources between the corporate marketing department and the corporate library. In this particular case, there were two internal champions: a corporate librarian with a strong library science background and extensive data base searching skills and a manager in corporate marketing with the organizational clout and budget necessary to finance and implement an intelligence network. The company benefited from the fact that the library was already the setting for many information sources and department personnel were already finely attuned to information management skills and data base searching.

Upper management favored this coordinated effort between corporate marketing and the library for four reasons:

1. Such a coordinated effort would promote the notion of interdepartmental teamwork, which benefits the organization as a whole.
2. The involvement of both departments would increase the level of user input and feedback to the network.
3. The project would be an enhancement of an existing department, rather than the creation of a new department or function.
4. Pooled resources would reduce duplication of effort

and the number of man-hours needed to implement the system.

Additional Criteria for Choosing a Department

Although there is no clear-cut guideline as to which department or functional area should be responsible for developing and maintaining a shared information network, there are some important criteria to consider.

1. Pick a department that is already a viable source of business and competitive information for either all or a significant part of the organization. Thus, the department should have a strong knowledge of the organization and the competitive and business events that affect the company. Although the corporate library or information center represents an ideal setting in many organizations, both large and small, it may take a coordinated effort between this function and another department that has more ready access to the current activities of the organization.

2. Choose a department that can work well with other departments and whose personnel have excellent communication skills. This becomes very important when the department is trying to "sell" a shared information network to other departments and senior management. These skills are also important if you are part of a small division of a large organization or if you are the only person responsible for gathering information in a small organization.

3. If there are various departments that could be the setting for a shared information network, choose one that is very forward thinking, results oriented, and respected throughout the organization. Thus, department personnel should be willing to withstand the potential risk and pitfalls associated with a companywide information network.

Other Responsibilities of the Intelligence Network Department

The department or functional area responsible for a corporate intelligence network may serve a number of other functions. The department may act as a liaison to external information suppliers, consulting firms, and research firms. In some instances, the department may even establish a competitive or business information hot line. This allows personnel from other departments to tap the resources of the department by telephone or computer. The department may even publish a monthly or weekly internal newsletter that highlights key business and competitive events.

What Type of Information Should Be Part of a Shared Information Network?

Most corporations are interested in keeping their employees informed of the key competitive or business events that affect their products or services. In today's business environment, most executives are finding an increased need for actionable information and global information. This information can be readily available or new information that is not yet available. The key notion here is to centralize the key topic areas that are important to the organization. The following are broad topic areas needed by almost every type of business:*

Industry Trends	Industry trends are general tendencies or consistent directions in a given market or industry. For instance, a trend in the food industry is the tremendous amount of consolidation and reorganization among supermarket chains.
Environmental Trends	Demographic and socioeconomic factors strongly affect the business environment. Examples of such trends are the growing elderly segment, the influx of dual income families, and the convenience-oriented society of today.

---

*Examples of each of these topic areas are highlighted in Appendixes A through G. These Appendixes focus on different industries or markets.

Legislative and Regulatory Events	Government regulations have become an increasing concern of corporations. Now more than ever, businesses are affected by local, state, and federal governments, as well as regulatory agencies such as the Food and Drug Administration and the Securities and Exchange Commission.
Competitor Activity	More and more organizations are systematically monitoring the activities of their competitors.
Product Development	Whether it be a new type of ready-to-eat cereal or a new patented process for the development of a fat substitute, organizations are demanding real-time information on new products.
Mergers and Acquisitions	With merger mania still rampant, organizations have become financial prey to their peer organizations, leveraged buyout concerns, and stock brokerage houses. Acquisitions have sensitized some organizations to a point where their strategic objective is to remain independent.
International Events	In today's global business environment, many multinational organizations have beefed up their overseas operations and are looking to new areas for growth. International events will affect many businesses, especially as trade barriers continue to fall in Europe and parts of Asia.

The challenge facing executives is to organize the universe of external information along with their internal information within these broad topic areas in relation to their line of business. In many organizations, file folders serve this purpose quite well. However, a growing number of corporations are designing systems that effectively integrate internal and external information. These systems are discussed in more detail in Chapter 7.

Format of the Information

An electronic data base or computerized system containing copy file folders allows users to search several topic areas or file folders. Commercial data base publishers generate information on a wide variety of topics and use sophisticated software to enable the user to retrieve the information through key word search techniques and other methods. Many managers need some type of customized corporate filing system or intelligence data base with which to access information. Such a data base should provide synthesized information from a wide variety of textual sources that are relevant to the operations of the organization.

Hard Copy

If you are employed in a small company that does not have access to a personal or mainframe computer, you can construct your own intelligence data base in hard copy. Many companies have a library that catalogs internal information and keeps relevant records for the company. Although file folders help a company keep hard copy files for its records, access or retrieval of the information can become difficult as these files grow in size. A hard copy data base design may suffice under any of the following scenarios:

- The organization is small and the decision makers are few.
- The products and services offered are few and very specialized.
- The competitors are few and well-defined.
- The business, competitive, and environmental fac-

tors that affect the organization are very stable and do not change much over time.

Electronic Format

With the advent of the personal computer and the increasing storage capabilities in desk-top equipment, many companies are looking toward a corporate intelligence data base customized to their needs. Electronic format of the information enables users to pull up the information on a computer screen, and sophisticated text retrieval software enables end users to search through the data base in an efficient manner.

In many cases, an organization develops an information network in which a hard copy format parallels the information in electronic format. Such a design works well for several reasons. It gives the network consistency and continuity. Also, incorporating hard copy and electronic forms satisfies the information needs of a wider audience. For instance, many mid- to senior-level executives do not have the time or even desire to read important information on a computer screen. So a hard copy approach works well. On the other hand, many managers who have data processing or library science backgrounds prefer to read information from computer screens.

Design of the Data Base

The design of a corporate intelligence data base is the most important element of the system. Some companies spend millions of dollars on elaborate corporate intelligence data bases only to find out that it is easier to use file drawers to retrieve the information than it is to navigate the data base. The data base, however, should reflect how the management of the organization views the business. Key variables such as the lines of business, competitors, markets, and products should be well thought out.

If a company has an objective to keep hundreds of its employees informed of key business events on a daily, weekly, or monthly basis, electronic information networks most efficiently store and disseminate this type of information. On the other hand, if the company is a moderate-size firm, the circulation of a daily news sheet or weekly or monthly newsletter may be more effective.

In a growing number of corporate settings, senior managers are becoming the most viable end users of intelligence networks that are derived from a variety of internal and external sources. To meet the need of the executive to pull information from diverse sources, the notion of executive information systems (EISs) evolved. These systems, which are networked using personal computers, allow senior managers to monitor and control large, geographically dispersed, and complex organizations. Although such systems are effective, the utility of EIS needs to be distributed to the departments or functional areas of an organization.

In a certain respect, many corporate departments or functional areas of an organization serve as an information broker with the operating divisions or field operations. Because their function dictates that they gather information from and feed information back to the business units, they are the best end users of a corporate intelligence network.

Distribution of the Information

Clearly, shared information networks increase in complexity with the increase in information stored and the increase in dissemination to diverse and multiple departments. The most effective shared information networks encompass extensive organization, synthesis, and digestion of the information prior to distribution to select departments. The following story from one company describes such a situation.

Designing an Effective Shared Information Network

A large parent company was faced with the task of gathering and disseminating timely and relevant information to diverse operating divisions. This objective was complicated by the fact that the parent company and operating companies had considerably diverse product lines, on a domestic and worldwide basis.

To accomplish the task, the corporate marketing department assumed the role of internal champion and, with the assistance of an outside consultant, conducted an extensive strategic information audit. The audit revealed that both managers and executives had a need for a shared information network that contained the following information categories:

- General business/environmental information
- Specific competitor information, organized by line of business
- International competitive information
- Internal documents relevant to the aforementioned categories

Moreover, the information had to be scanned, digested, and put into the system on a daily basis, for access the next morning. How did the firm accomplish this objective? One of the first steps taken by corporate marketing was to schematically design the optimum shared information network from the results of the strategic information audit (see Figure 2-2).

Following development of the schematic, corporate marketing, with the assistance of corporate information systems and an outside consulting firm, developed a prototype and installed the data on a flexible, mainframe text retrieval package. A systematic schedule was then developed for users to log into the system. One of the keys to success of the system was an extensive feedback process that corporate marketing built into the system. The system included the installation of an electronic mail function that allowed end users to provide feedback on the system, give comments or highlight information that was on the system, and communicate with the outside consulting firm. This process was conducted on a continuous basis and had support from the operating units.

Figure 2-2. Shared information network design.

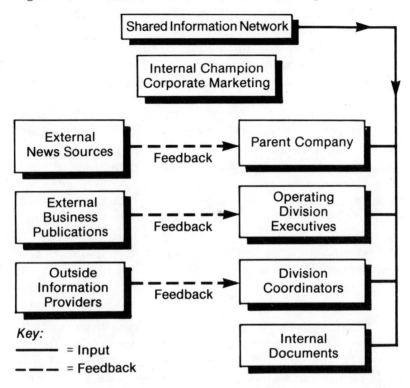

Bottom Line Impact. The operating divisions in newly developed markets gained rapid access to business and technical information that enabled them to accelerate their product development cycle.

The mature operating divisions now had an organized process by which to monitor their competition on an ongoing basis. The greatest value was derived from information on competitors in the Far East.

Reduced duplication of effort was cited in areas of new business or market development projects.

Resource Requirements

There is no doubt that these systems require at least one central coordinator. This position is responsible for:

- Procurement of data sources (working with outside suppliers and internal suppliers of information)
- Maintenance of the data base
- Coordination of the feedback process
- End-user training
- Future growth enhancements to the network

In addition to these administrative and maintenance-based duties, the central coordinator must develop and nurture a reasonable level of awareness in peers and upper management. There are several ways the central coordinator may increase awareness. One way is to develop an in-house promotional effort. This may include brochures, promotional flyers, or even interoffice memos that are distributed to intended users of the system and highlight the benefits of the system. The coordinator should emphasize the benefits most suited to the user's needs. They might include the following:

- The system is simple to master and user friendly, even to users who are not very computer literate.
- The system will dramatically reduce duplication of effort and reduce or eliminate the need for external news sources or publications.
- The system encourages information sharing and discourages information hoarding.
- The system systematically monitors competition.
- The system provides synthesis and analysis and contains the information that is most relevant to the activities of the organization.

The central coordinator may set up actual demonstrations of the system for peers and senior management. Such an interactive process should give an excellent indication whether awareness can be turned into acceptance. It also should result in some kind of feedback report that the central coordinator gives to management. These demonstrations should take place when all the "bugs" are out of the system.

In addition to developing an awareness level, the coordinator must also be a good salesperson of the system. Unless the users are aware of the information product and service offerings and enhancements to the system, they are dealing with a "blind spot." In some cases, two or more administrative people may be required to assist the central coordinator in large shared information networks, particularly those that are global in scope.

How to Measure the Effectiveness of the Network

According to Citibank, its system "brings the efficiencies of a flat organization without Citibank being one."[1] These benefits—the ability to quantify productivity savings, block a competitor's moves, or bring a product to market quicker—illustrate the effectiveness of the system. There should be a thorough semiannual review of a network, rather than a quarterly review, to allow a time frame long enough to pinpoint tangible benefits or savings. Typically, such a review entails the use of hard copy questionnaires or personal interviews.

For organizations that have developed an intelligence network, the effectiveness of the network can be measured by answering the following questions:

- Are the goals and potential benefits of the network well-communicated?
- Does the network have support from top management and several key functional areas (for instance, field sales, market research)?
- Can the network be modified or adjusted as the objectives and goals of the organization change?
- Are the people involved in the development or on-

---

[1] Reprinted from the April 27, 1988, issue of *The BusinessWeek Newsletter for Information Executives* by special permission, Copyright © 1988 by McGraw-Hill, Inc.

going maintenance of the network motivated? Do
they generate new ideas?

- Does the network effectively and efficiently gather
  and disseminate intelligence?
- Does the network provide pertinent information that
  can be transformed into actionable decision making?
- Does the network contain built-in measures for obtaining feedback?
- Are there provisions for reviewing and evaluating the
  network on a systematic basis?

Pitfalls

One pitfall of an intelligence network is failure of users to
limit the amount of information that is loaded into the
system; some people have the urge to integrate way too
much information. Another pitfall can open up if the system initially involves too many groups or users at once. The
execution of these systems is important. A phased development, in terms of both information content and end-user
involvement, is recommended. Also, if the system is not
being used, find out why. Perhaps another route, as indicated by the following company's story, might be more
successful.

An Integrated Electronic and Hard Copy Network

A corporate librarian from a midsize integrated services
digital network equipment firm wants to develop a hard
copy information tool that is channeled to key executives of
the organization. Given the size of the company (fewer than
1,000 employees), communication is not a critical factor. In
this approach, the main challenge is to gather and digest
information from hundreds of external sources, with limited resources. The librarian realizes that building an electronic information network is unnecessary and, from a
budgetary perspective, impossible. What is needed, however, is a device that communicates external environmental
intelligence to key executives.

The librarian realizes that a hard copy reporting system or newsletter might be more appropriate. The librarian clearly maps out a schematic or blueprint of the hard copy reporting system. The schematic defines the purpose of the system, notes the intended users, and provides a mechanism for continuous feedback. The newsletter or hard copy reporting system, however, can still contain the same information elements as an electronic network.

The information obtained for such a newsletter may be gathered from daily publications, industry-specific or trade publications, and the field (sales representatives). Typically, sources would be included as part of the newsletter because many readers might want to refer to the original article. Such a newsletter may be set up for distribution on a weekly, biweekly, or even monthly basis. In some cases, an intelligence newsletter may be updated on a daily basis. Examples of such newsletters are detailed in Appendixes H and I.

Summary

The first step in developing a shared information network is to approach your colleagues about the concept. Overall, the concept may involve input from various departments, including marketing research, information systems, finance, corporate library, or even legal. The key factor for you to discuss is the impact of a shared information network within your organization. You may want to schedule a one-hour meeting to brainstorm what the schematic would look like. The more departments involved in the conceptual/planning phase, the more successful the system will be. Use the topics that have been discussed in this chapter as the agenda for the meeting. Keep in mind these key questions:

Why develop a shared information network?
Is there a system already in place?
What are the critical information needs of our organization?

What are our critical lines of business?
What should the network look like?
Who are the users?
Who will be responsible?
What are the potential pitfalls?
What budgetary questions are there?

For any phased process, such as the development of a shared information network, meetings that attempt to answer these questions are critical to the success of the network. Chapter 3 discusses the phases involved in developing an information network.

3

How to Get Started

"The biggest problem is deciding how and where to start an intelligence network."

Ed Rubinstein, Project Director, Strategic Intelligence
Systems, Inc.

By now you are probably thinking that a business intelligence network sounds great and is exactly what your department or company needs to become an "intelligent" organization. You may be asking the question, How do I get started? Again, the need for and benefits of this type of program depend on senior management support and a coordinated effort of several departments. Sometimes, one department in a corporation will successfully initiate its own program or system. After the department has attained a desired level of awareness and installed a working system that is constantly evolving, other departments see the value in the system and either want a similar one or want to share in the information network.

This chapter contains a series of steps, eleven in all, that tell how to develop a business intelligence network. Each step involves a certain investment in what has become the most closely monitored element in today's business environment—time. As the steps are outlined, we look at actual corporations that have developed a business or corporate intelligence network in one form or another.

Because business intelligence networks are new to organizations, there are no set methodologies to initiate them. They all require, however, the elements discussed in the eleven steps, in one form or another. Some organizations have successfully developed a business intelligence network, some have stagnated at a certain phase, and others have not even started. If you are actively involved in developing such a network, you may want to use these steps as a benchmark for what has been completed and what still needs to be done.

Step 1: Identify the Internal Champion

Someone has to assume the role of internal champion to implement the corporate intelligence system. Having observed several executives functioning in this capacity, I can assure you that the task is not an easy one.

The success of a corporate intelligence network is dependent on the ability of the internal champion to coordinate with senior- and middle-level executives in the operating divisions, the marketing research staff, the planning staff, the information systems staff, and other functional areas such as research and development and manufacturing. Internal champions frequently emerge from the following functional areas:

- Strategic planning
- Corporate marketing
- Marketing research
- Controller's office
- Information systems
- Research and development
- Manufacturing
- Corporate development

Recently, the title "chief information officer" (CIO) has been placed on many organization charts. Generally, CIOs are likely to be the best internal champions. With the need for global and field intelligence, the function of the CIO will be critical to organizations during the 1990s and beyond.

You may be the internal champion or you may identify someone on your staff who should have the responsibility for developing an intelligence network. The internal champion should have the following seven attributes:

1. *Strong leadership ability.* The internal champion should be perceived by senior management, peers, and subordinates as an innovator and a doer.

2. *Excellent communication skills.* The internal champion must articulate the need for and benefits of the system.
3. *Company knowledge.* The internal champion must have an in-depth knowledge of the organization, the organization's products or services, and its business environment.
4. *Results-oriented philosophy.* A results-oriented approach is necessary to demonstrate the cost savings or additional revenues that can be generated from an intelligence network.
5. Vision. *Because intelligence networks evolve and are constantly changing, the internal champion must have the vision to shape and mold the system according to the changing objectives of the organization.*
6. *Sales ability.* Strong sales skills are necessary to "market" the system to other departments internally and attract more users. In addition, the internal champion may even be the one who markets or promotes the system outside the organization and to the media.
7. *Willingness to take risks.* The internal champion must be willing to accept either the success or failure of the system.

As you read this book, ask yourself the question, Who should be the internal champion of this effort in our company? The most successful efforts have been undertaken by individuals who recognized the need themselves rather than those to whom the job was delegated by a superior. Once the champion is identified and these objectives are built into his or her job function, the following steps must be taken.

Step 2: Organize the Internal Effort

Given the nature of these systems, their success or failure is contingent on the ability of the internal champion to marshal the efforts of key people in corporate staff or operating divisions. Although each situation may differ, the following functional areas are typically involved in the effort:

- Strategic planning
- Marketing research
- Controller's office
- Information systems
- Corporate library
- Operating division management

Once the internal champion has identified the departments that would use the intelligence network, the specific uses they would make of the network and the information they would load into it must be determined. Thus, the internal champion may want to identify the information management roles of these departments. The three following questions should be asked:

1. What are the primary responsibilities of your function or department?
2. How are these responsibilities affected by information?
3. How does your function or department make use, if any, of information that can affect your responsibilities?

Table 3-1 shows sample information management roles of the input departments. Note that all these departments use information for decision-making purposes, in one form or another.

When the information management roles of departments that will use the network have been identified, the internal champion should select key company personnel or even an outside consultant to assist in developing the shared information network. The champion and this select group of key personnel comprise the task force that oversees the internal effort of the system.

Once the departmental infrastructure and the information management roles of the input departments have been identified and the task force has been organized, a work plan should be developed.

Table 3-1.   Sample information management roles.

Department	Information Management Roles
Strategic Planning	Actively involved in gathering competitive intelligence and obtaining information that is consistent with the strategic objectives of the organization (for example, entering a new market)
	Concerned with information that has an impact on the long-term goals of the organization and its competitive environment
	Relies on the information-gathering functions of other departments within the organization or hires experts in this area
Marketing Research	Actively involved in gathering information that directly pertains to the market research function, such as market share data, test results of new products, demographics, and psychographics
	Actively involved in monitoring environmental information that affects the organization, such as societal trends
	Becoming more involved in obtaining information from and distributing information to those departments that do not work in corporate environments (for example, field sales, R&D, manufacturing)
Controller's Office	Gathers information that will increase company productivity and result in cost savings
Information Systems	Becoming more involved in obtaining information from and distributing information to those departments that do not work in corporate environments (field sales, R&D, manufacturing, and so on)

(continued)

Table 3-1. (continued)

Department	Information Management Roles
Information Systems, con't.	Actively involved in gathering information for the sales and marketing functions of the organization (for example, market share statistics, sales data obtained from universal product code scanners)
	Gathers information from many other departments and ties them into one efficient information system
Corporate Library	Provides business research for all functions within the organization and searches commercial on-line data bases
	Becoming more involved in capturing relevant information from secondary sources to develop internally published documents, such as newsletters
Division Management	Actively involved in obtaining relevant information that pertains to the business of the division

Step 3: Develop a Work Plan

The work plan serves as a conceptual time frame for the development of a corporate intelligence network. It may also entail organizing a task force to develop such a plan. The most successful business intelligence networks are executed against a well-thought-out work plan that secures a commitment from senior management. In addition, the plan should be based on the immediate and long-term objectives of the organization.

How many times has your company embarked on the development of a new process or system, only to find out, hundreds of thousands of dollars later, that a simple, less complex process would have sufficed? Because corporate intelligence systems are still a "blind spot," it is wise to proceed cautiously and implement a phased approach. Many of my clients term this process a "pilot" project, and should the system be successful, then incremental investments are made. Costs can be carefully controlled through a phased approach as follows:

Phase I.	Diagnosis of End-User Needs
Phase II.	Analysis of Needs
Phase III.	Design of the Prototype
Phase IV.	End-User Feedback of the Prototype
Phase V.	Implementation of the System

This type of phased approach, with objectives and deliverables plotted against specific time frames, allows management to "pull the plug" at the end of any phase, before further costly development. Table 3-2 gives details of a sample work plan. Chapter 12 discusses in detail tying the system to the bottom line.

Historically, many corporations have attempted to set up a shared information network without the assistance of external consultants. For the sample plan shown in Table 3-2, the time factors involved the assistance of an outside firm. For those organizations that "go it alone," it may take longer to complete each phase.

Step 4: Begin the Planning Phase

During this phase, a series of meetings should be held to identify short- and long-term goals for the system. These discussions should be well thought out and strategic in scope, that is, they should be based on the immediate and long-term objectives of the organization. The more streamlined this process is, the less likely it will be put off.

In some organizations, "task force paralysis" occurs. In this scenario, the internal champion has been identified and a work plan has been mapped out, but the planning phase has been stymied by corporate bottlenecks. Such pitfalls are described later in this chapter. The planning phase should be executed in a four- to six-week time frame with a brief

Table 3-2.   Sample work plan.

Phase	Tasks/Objectives	Time Frame
I. End-User Needs	Task force schedules interviews with key management or potential users of the system. The interviews should ■ assess the current information-gathering activities ■ list current information sources that are used, measure the utility of these sources, and develop a "wish list" of expanded information sources ■ discuss the expected access to and frequency of use of the system ■ reveal the desired format of the information, timeliness of the information, and frequency of update of the system	Approximately 1 month
II. Needs Analysis	Upon completion of the interviews, the task force analyzes the information obtained and develops one or a series of conceptual designs for the shared information network.	1–2 weeks
III. Prototype	Upon widespread approval of the conceptual and technical design of the system, the task force develops a prototype.	1 month

Phase	Tasks/Objectives	Time Frame
IV. Feedback	During the next 30-day period the task force assists users in accessing the system and obtains end-user feedback. During this phase, the objective is to make any necessary changes to the system indicated by this feedback.	1 month
V. Implementation	When end-user feedback has been obtained and incorporated into the system, the task force then puts the network into "publication." During this "shakeout" period, the task force may work closely with the department to continue to make refinements to the system. As indicated by the interviews (Phase I), the information content of the system can be updated on a daily, weekly, biweekly, or monthly basis.	2–3 months

planning document or PERT chart representing the deliverables to senior management.

Step 5: Conduct the Strategic Information Audit

The strategic information audit is discussed in detail in Chapter 4. This phase should entail conducting internal interviews, analyzing the results, and presenting the findings to senior management. Depending upon the availability of internal executives, this phase should take between four and six weeks. The deliverable is a cohesive document that analyzes the survey results, along with a "blueprint" or information architecture of the corporate intelligence network.

Step 6: Develop a Prototype

Rome was not built in a day. Neither will be a corporate intelligence system. These systems should be designed with significant flexibility to accommodate changes in the corporation and its lines of business. Ideally, business intelligence systems should integrate both internal and external information. Thus, prototyping is absolutely necessary to determine if the system is flexible enough to meet the short- and long-term needs of the company. Such a system is a strategic intelligence network.

The prototype for a business intelligence network acts as a small-scale offering or test market of the network. At this point, the internal champion and the task force must decide whether to develop the prototype in-house or hire an outside firm. The average time frame for this process is four to six weeks.

End users also should be involved in the design and development of the prototype. Just as a manager or administrator would set up his or her own filing system to be able to find specific information, the users of the system should have input into the content and format of the data base. The company's story that follows underscores this notion of end-user buy-in.

Management Information Systems Myopia

The management information systems (MIS) department of a large financial institution had a mission to develop a corporate intelligence system containing internal documents and external strategic and competitive intelligence information. Although the project director of the MIS department met with and interviewed the vice-president and directors of planning, marketing, and finance, she did not interview middle-level management and administrative end users of the data base. More important, a significant financial commitment was made to purchase expensive "glitzy" software that promised to be all things to all people. Following the purchase and installation of the software, MIS management began to search for information to put into the data base. Little or no planning had been conducted at the outset as to the strategic information content requirement, profile of the end users, format of the information, frequency of update of the information, and so on. As a result, this department became saddled with expensive costs in search of a useful application, illustrating why input and buy-in are essential for the successful implementation of these systems.

Because of cost and time constraints, prototyping is best executed on a personal computer. Following a thirty- to forty-five-day interview period or audit, the prototype should be developed during the next thirty days. Whether the prototype is implemented on a personal computer or the corporate mainframe, software should be selected and the design of the format and a selection of information should be loaded into the computer during this time period. Timing is important because the project may lose momentum if management has to wait three to six months to view the system.

Give the End Users Something to Play With

A few years ago, my firm designed and developed a prototype of an intelligence system that synthesized and summarized more than 1,500 internal documents of a corporation. Following interviews with several layers of staff, we realized that senior management had a view of the system that differed significantly from that of middle-level management and the potential system administrators. With this diversity of opinion, we developed at least three alternative designs of the data base and small-scale prototypes of the system within two weeks to enable each level of management to "play with the system" prior to further development. This method proved invaluable because we had more than 1,500 documents to synthesize and load into the system during the next six to eight weeks. The feedback from these early prototypes enabled us to change the design of the data base prior to costly data input.

Data base prototyping should be kept simple. Corporations that attempt to develop an "omnibus" approach to data bases experience resistance from various levels of management, in addition to low system usage. Prototypes should solve no more than two to three objectives. Some sample objectives of prototypes include the following:

Prototype Objectives

- Develop a bibliographic capturing of internal documents.
- Include a brief summary of the content of internal documents.
- Develop a data base searchable by key word.
- Design a new-product-development tracking system.
- Profile the data base by line of business and geographic region.
- Integrate internal and external information.
- Design a market research automated library.
- Include bibliographic information of purchased studies.
- Include a synthesis of the external literature.

Automation Market Research

One of the most successful systems I developed was the automation of a market research library for a major money center bank. Like most market research functions, the market research department has a hard copy library of purchased syndicated studies, customized studies, industry periodicals, internally generated reports, and a plethora of other market-research-specific files (results from focus group sessions, surveys, clippings of competitors' ads, research from ad firms, and so on).

Because there were three administrators of this project and each one had a different view of what the documents should look like, it was my task to put commonality to the documents. My mission was to develop a prototype that would satisfy personnel who were very detail oriented and those who were less detail oriented.

Phase I of the project focused on capturing relevant information in a one-page or one-screen summary. As a result, my firm's team of document analysts synthesized and analyzed the library's documents and extracted the following information elements. Although the elements were the actual field titles, the information within each field is fictional for this example.

Example:	One-Screen "Intelligence" Summary
Code:	GA01101
Title:	Survey—Regional Usage of Automated Teller Machines
Author/Sponsor:	XYZ Research Company, Inc.
Date:	September 12, 1988
Summary:	The purpose of this study was to use qualitative research to track the usage patterns of automated teller machines (ATMs) on a regional basis.
Implications:	The study found that ATM usage was heavily concentrated on the East and West Coasts and in the Southeast, but was less frequent in the Midwest and Southwest. For action(s) taken on the basis of this study, contact Ms. Florence McIntyre at extension 4130.
Cross-Reference/Key Words:	ATM, Regional, XYZ Research

Although some companies may have a market research library, usually the information may not be accessible by other departments or field locations. The design of a simple system that catalogs this type of information can give a company a competitive advantage by allowing access to all this information in one centralized location. The design and development of this type of system for the bank gave it a clear competitive edge over its competition. For instance, before spending additional funds on market research for new product development, it would search the data base to determine whether a study had been conducted on the subject. This eliminated costly duplication of research for new products, which could actually become extensions of existing products.

Following the design of the prototype, the internal champion, in conjunction with the task force, should select the initial content for the system. Clearly, this should be "high-impact, high-payoff material" derived from a wide variety of information sources, yet filtered of information not relevant to the organization.

Step 7: Obtain User Feedback

Following the development of a prototype and selection of the initial content of the intelligence network, the internal champion or the task force must obtain end-user feedback and make modifications to the system, where and if necessary. Such modifications may include allowing for refinements of the actual format and data base design. For instance, many executives prefer information that is summarized by key points, rather than in general prose or paragraph form. The different types of data base design are discussed later in this chapter.

In assessing the prototype, users may want to add more information sources or delete sources deemed unnecessary. This type of feedback underscores the value of integrating internal and external information into the network. Chapter 7, "Building the System," contains a discussion of this process.

Although some users may find the prototype of the intelligence network informative, in some instances they think the information on the network insults their intelligence. Hypothetically, this might result in the question, How do you convince the product manager of a leading national brand that a business intelligence network will improve his function and bottom line profits? This is not an easy assignment for the internal champion and the task force and is where the notion of value-added information services comes into play. Generally, a business intelligence network increases in value when the information includes some form of analysis, which transforms a shared information network into a business intelligence network or strategic intelligence system. This analysis might answer the following questions:

- What might this event or news mean for the company?
- What might this event or news mean for the business unit that I represent?
- How might our organization or our competitors respond to this event or news?
- What other departments or functional areas might be affected by this event or news?

Such analysis may be performed by the group responsible for the prototype network. In today's business environment, however, a growing number of organizations are using the services of external information suppliers. The initial feedback of the system best serves the internal champion and the task force with a formal survey distributed to the end users of the network. The following is a sample of what such a survey might look like:

General

1. How often do you access the network?
2. Do you access the system on a systematic basis (daily, weekly, biweekly)?
3. Do you find the system to be user friendly?

Content/Format

4. What are your general comments about the system (format, timeliness, depth and breadth of information sources)?
5. Has the system met your expectations? If not, explain.
6. Has the system affected your line of business or job function?
7. What type of information did you find useful? Not useful?
8. Is there additional information you think should be included in the network? If so, what information?

After the survey is distributed and routed back to the task force, the next step is to quantify the comments to make concrete changes to the system. The changes may be extensive or minimal. After the changes are incorporated, the task force should utilize telephone follow-up procedures to "keep everyone happy."

Typically, the task force should distribute a formal survey to the end users on an annual basis, at least. In addition, telephone follow-up surveys should be made every ninety days. It is important to realize that although feedback from the initial prototype may take three to four weeks, the feedback loop is an ongoing process and will continue throughout the life of the system.

Step 8: Develop the System

Following the development of a prototype, it is appropriate to select the hardware and software if management determines such an information system should be developed. If the prototype was successful, this phase may involve transferring data to a large-scale computerized system. This phase should also include the training of select users of the system. The person chosen to train the users should be a member of the task force and may be called the systems coordinator.

The systems coordinator should have a small staff (two to three people) and also work with the internal champion in training select users. Ideally, the staff of the systems coordinator would include a technical support person who trains end users and a marketer of the system who acts as a "hand holder" or internal customer service representative (see Figure 3-1).

The estimated time frame to execute step 8 is approximately three months.

Step 9: Roll Out the System

Once the system is in place, additional users should be added. In this phase a communications program should be developed to increase the number of participants. The communications program need not be expensive. The following are some suggestions for communications programs for the system:

- Presentations to senior management
- A corporate newsletter that highlights the system

Figure 3-1. Relationship of systems coordinator to staff.

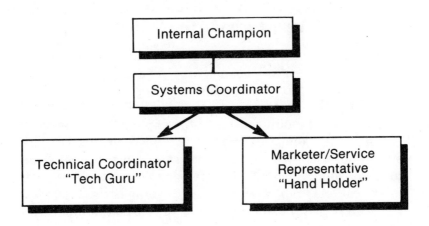

- A minidemonstration or marketing scheme that is accessed by personal computer or floppy disk
- Demonstrations at company conferences

A User-Friendly Communications Package

A major bank creatively implemented a totally integrated communications package on a floppy disk. To encourage access to a valuable strategic information data base, the internal champion and his task force ensured that the system was easy to access, especially for those who were not personal computer–literate. Such a simple connection to the system eliminated user frustration found with traditional communications software. The bank then developed a floppy disk that connected the user directly to the system. This floppy disk also had user-friendly and eye-appealing graphics, the corporate logo, and system name. Users comment that the system is "fun to use."

During this phase, additional users should be signed on to the business intelligence network to realize its benefits and derive leverage from investment in the data base or system. As more users are signed on to the system, a system support structure that services the users must be put into place.

Step 10: Establish a Support Structure for the System

A support structure evolves over time and is critical to the long-term success of the network. The support structure contains a help or service function built into the system that assists the internal champion in handling user feedback and allows for modifications to the content of the network. As more valuable information is added to the network, additional users will access the system. This support structure constantly entails user feedback and can result in modifications to the system on an ongoing basis.

At a relatively simple level, a support structure for the

system can be put into place by establishing two components:

1. A job function or department within the organization that is responsible for providing users with system support, in essence a troubleshooting function
2. A "hot line" that users can telephone for technical support and for assistance with information content

In most organizations, the actual support structure of a shared information network is either small or nonexistent. In some organizations, however, such a support system can be quite large and sophisticated. In Chapter 7 we examine how a unit within Ford Motor Company successfully implemented that company's system by use of a support structure.

Step 11: Promote Evolution of the System

Strategic intelligence systems or networks involve continuous evaluation and modification. Because they are tied to the business environment and are content-driven, they must be continually changing. Moreover, the internal champion is often slated for a new job function (oftentimes a promotion) following the execution of such a system. Thus, it is important that the internal champion train a successor during this one- to two-year implementation period.

Pitfalls

These eleven steps sound so easy. Having personally executed them, I can honestly say that this is not an easy task. However, these systems have demonstrated bottom line results and are viewed by many organizations as necessary for long-term success. Although some pitfalls may seem like major obstacles, the actual cases presented throughout this book reveal that major corporations have overcome them.

The point here is to be aware of the potential pitfalls and develop a strategy to deal with them.

Lack of a Budget

If you have identified yourself as the internal champion and you have sold the idea to senior management, you must secure some type of budget approval. If you are charged with implementing this task without a budget—good luck. It is better to defer implementing the project until either a certain department, business unit, or division will support the project or until you can obtain funding in the next budget cycle.

Internal "Green-Eyed Monsters"

Suppose you have a budget for this project and another department (say, the corporate library) perceives this corporate intelligence network as a threat to its traditional function or as an invasion of its "turf." It is best to dispel these internal turf wars at the beginning of the project. It should be articulated to other staff groups or divisions that this is a shared information network that will benefit all groups.

In one intelligence network that I helped set up for the information systems division of a Fortune 100 firm, internal "green-eyed monsters" sprouted from various departments, including the corporate library, the division marketing research department, and the corporate marketing research department. In such cases, I suggest that you take the following early warning indicators into consideration:

- During the needs analysis process or the strategic information audit, attempt to establish participation from various departments. This may increase acceptance.
- Although some of the internal interviews may be quite formal, the internal champion and the task force may find it worthwhile to conduct informal interviews with personnel from those departments

that appear the most likely to have green-eyed monsters.

■ Although the internal champion and the task force may receive a lot of credit from top management for the system, this group must realize that corporate culture is involved. Thus, it is their responsibility to cite any monsters at the earliest stage possible.

Unfortunately, sometimes this fear cannot be dispelled until you have reached step 8 or 9. At this point, some of the most resistant departments become some of the strongest champions of the system.

"Not Invented Here" Syndrome

Corporate egos often give rise to a "not invented here" syndrome. This happens when personnel actually fear what top management would say if told "an outside firm developed the prototype" or "we are doing about 25 percent of the work in-house." As a result, many organizations have decided to go it alone. Unfortunately, this can be quite costly and even negatively affect the business. I am familiar with a company that decided to develop its corporate intelligence network solely with its internal resources. Although among them the employees of this corporation had just about every type of skill available, they were unfamiliar with the nuances involved in the development of this type of system. After a two-year effort costing over $500,000 in manpower, an approach was pursued that involved outside assistance.

Compiling information data bases, which is the most valuable component of a shared information network, entails very specific skills. Most corporate managers and executives do not have time to scan, organize, and summarize information because they are required to spend time in meetings, on the phone, and analyzing information for the purpose of making decisions. Furthermore, it is unrealistic to expect full-time dedication to your project or data base when key people are employed by other divisions or departments. Given this fact of corporate life, the internal champion will have to develop a game plan incorporating a workable solution to this potential pitfall. In many instances, he or she will need help from the outside.

Security Issues

It is clear that a business intelligence network may contain valuable and highly sensitive information. The last thing you want is to have any of this information end up in the hands of a competitor. Whether a corporate intelligence network consists of hard copy files or an electronic data base, security procedures and measures must be strictly enforced.

All corporations face the issue of an employee who leaves the firm and goes to work for a competitor. For years, corporations have developed specific policies and have worked with their legal staffs to protect their interests in this area. With the new age of computer systems, personal computers, and electronic information, the issue of corporate security is magnified. Thus, the development of an information network, which may contain internally generated information on competitive intelligence, product development strategy, or market performance, requires strict security procedures.

The internal champion and the task force dedicated to the project must work out a series of security procedures consistent with corporate policies and standard or generally accepted legal procedures. The following are some of the security measures that can be implemented:

- Issue controlled user-identification numbers that limit access to the system.
- Have a third-party vendor maintain the data base.
- Employ an administrator to maintain strict procedures of access to the system if personal computers are used.
- Lock up floppy disks.
- Document procedures for controlled downloading of information from the system.

- Partition the data base, whereby some sections can be accessed by the entire user population and some sections or topic areas can only be accessed by controlled user groups.
- Develop a monitoring system that tracks individual and group user frequency.
- Remove user-identification number immediately upon notification of employee termination or relocation to another firm.
- Restrict printing of files or limit printing of information.

Although many of these procedures may discourage widespread use of the system, they can be explained and enforced in the form of hard copy materials. The potential pitfall of security issues needs to be addressed during the planning and development phase of the system. Even so, for large corporate information networks that are global in scope, it may be necessary to balance security and accountability.

Balancing Security and Accountability

There are two possible ways to partition the network in a way that balances security with accountability. Both cases may require that the organization's legal department become well-attuned to what goes into the system. One way to partition the data base, both technically and conceptually, is according to specifications of the organization or functional area. For instance, a division within an organization may only have access to information that is relevant to the activities and competitive environment of that division.

The second way to balance security and accountability is to partition the data base on a "need to know" basis. In this case, data are separated by various levels of user groups. For instance, the top twenty or so executives of an organization may have access to information considered highly sensitive. This method of balancing security and accountability creates more of a hierarchy of users than partitioning the system by functional area.

System Stability

To properly execute the system, the internal champion should make at least a two-year commitment to the role of internal champion. Continuous rotation of staff to this position generates instability in the system. Similarly, the administrators of the system should also have at least a two-year commitment to their job functions.

One Company's Story

"We've evolved through four phases—first gathering competitive and market data, next performing competitive and market comparisons, then conducting competitive and market analysis, and finally, integrating these analyses into our strategic plan," says Martin Stark, Competitive Analysis Manager, strategic and market planning, AT&T.

Stark provides the following description of the business intelligence network that has been implemented at AT&T.

AT&T: A Large Corporation's Solution to Developing a Data Base

The job of our corporate staff group is to provide information and analysis to top corporate decision makers—particularly in the areas of markets and competitors. We have been building the required support structure from scratch as we moved from a regulated monopoly environment to a highly competitive environment.

At the start, we considered designing and developing a data base with all the data we might ever need on our competitors. We soon realized there were several problems with this approach. First of all—we were talking about an enormous data base, which would require substantial capital and personnel support cost. We were also faced with the problem of populating the data base, much less keeping it up to date. Finally, there was the challenge of providing analysis and recommendations—not just the data.

The approach we selected is to build a virtual data base—a distributed network of information and sources. We've integrated our network into the strategic planning process. And, we provide shared and ubiquitous access to the data. So, the strategic planning process and the specific support functions are each improved.

As big as AT&T is, we found many pockets of data and analysis in the operating business units. Our problem was networking between and among the experts. We built a sophisticated electronic Rolodex to provide our analysts with a network of AT&T subject matter experts for almost any given cross-section of subjects. We allow searches on products, services, companies, industries, and countries/regions. Companies include customers, competitors, distributors, and partners. Products and services range from broad categories to specific models.

In each operating unit, there are subject matter experts with current knowledge about our competitors and markets. Many of these experts maintain small (individual) data bases, which they keep up to date for their own job needs. From a corporate point of view, we incorporate that data, and the appropriate analysis/explanation, by maintaining our network of experts.

Our current version of the tool provides thesauruses to allow more robust information retrieval, mostly independent of terminology. We also use data networking to support electronic mail and broadcast mail capabilities. The information providers also benefit from access to our network. In other words, the participants share their information with us because we share our network with them.

AT&T has a variety of clipping services, both internal and external. Each service is focussed on a specific client group. For the strategic planners we use an electronic version, which adds value by including a competitive context statement provided by one of our subject matter experts.

Typically we have four to eight news items per day. The context statement describes why the news is strategically important and frequently includes recommended AT&T actions. We aim to publish by noon. We also maintain an archive which is used for tracking and trend analysis. We have a market characterization data base, which is sourced from our business unit experts. This single source of data provides consistency across our planning efforts. We have a consistent set of definitions, market size estimates, and estimated growth rates. We can cut the data by product category, customer set, or geography. We chose to centralize this data base to assure standardization.

We also collect and provide access to competitor financial data. Since we have many foreign competitors, and even domestically there are different reporting conventions, we devote substantial effort to normalizing and cleaning the data. We're addressing currency conversion rates, and a wide variety of discrepancies that show up in many external sources of financial data. Our operating units' financial analysis typically addresses comparable competitors' business units, as opposed to the enterprise view we take at corporate staff.

In conclusion, we've addressed the large data base problems of cost and timeliness by building a virtual or distributed network of data and sources, based on publicly available data. At each data source we have an expert who participates in the explanation and analysis of the data. And in the end, the whole is greater than the sum of the parts.

Summary

Clearly, not all companies are the size of AT&T or have such extensive resources. Also, not all organizations need to adhere religiously to the eleven steps outlined in this chapter. It is important for every organization, however, to get started in some way, shape, or form, through internal organizing and the concerted, cooperative efforts of its departments.

4

The Strategic Information Audit

"The focus of strategic information management is on having information you can use versus using information that you have."

J. Douglas Phillips, Senior Director, Corporate
Planning, Merck & Co., Inc.

Companies spend thousands and even millions of dollars on information and are not aware of the effectiveness of their investment. Information is becoming one of the most important assets of companies, both large and small. The challenge is to track not only the effectiveness of the information products that are purchased, but also the effectiveness of the process or information flow within a company. This is done by conducting an information audit.

The concept of an information audit is not new. Consulting firms have been applying this concept to traditional system development projects for some time. For years, companies have faced the challenge of tying their information plan to the strategic goals and objectives of the firm, a process that may be termed a "strategic information audit." In this chapter we examine the strategic information audit and document a top–down and a bottom–up assessment of the utility of information sources and systems within organizations. Rather than being based on a theoretical concept, this approach is based on projects that my firm and I have developed with companies facing these issues.

The Need for a Strategic Information Audit

A strategic information audit evaluates the effectiveness of an existing information system or network. The audit is critical because it can identify the strengths and weaknesses of a system. Specifically, it assesses the attitudes and practices of employees and management with respect to information sources and gathering and distributing information throughout the organization. The audit also evaluates current information channels and identifies what ought to be added to the system, as shown in the following:

Evaluates

- An existing system
- Current information needs
- Effectiveness of current information sources
- Effectiveness of information distribution and use of technology
- Information uses and needs by functional area or department

Identifies

- The information management objectives of the organization
- Information gaps, inconsistencies, or duplication of effort
- New information sources
- Possible amendments or changes to an existing system

During this phase of development, the internal champion, with the help of either an internal task force or external consultants, gathers a variety of opinions from colleagues and potential end users of the network. Oftentimes, a strategic information audit queries managers of many departments within an organization, including those departments that do not work at corporate headquarters (for example, field sales and manufacturing). Thus, when a large number of employees are queried in a strategic information audit, it gives the auditor a broad perspective. For instance, if a corporation has annual sales of $6 billion and employs about 2,000 at corporate headquarters and 8,000 in a sales or manufacturing function, the ideal number of interviews with key personnel would be between sixty and seventy. The results gained from such an involvement mix often generates new ideas for the information network.

You may be asking, With all my projects, committees, meetings, and so on, why tie up valuable resources for this task? Actually, many companies cannot afford *not* to initiate this task. Consider the following examples.

> Senior management is considering an acquisition in an industry or market that is unrelated to the base business. Timing is critical because several other firms may be involved in a bidding war for this company. You contact six departments internally to locate information on the specific company and related history. The information is incomplete. You contact several outside research firms for a bid on a "quick and dirty" study. You end up paying thousands of dollars for this study to find out that one of your foreign affiliates had an abundance of material on this company and the industry in its library. *The cost: inability to react quickly and unnecessary expenditures*

> Your division has been subscribing to the same information sources for years. Although these information sources are circulated quite efficiently throughout the organization, you ask the question, Does anyone read these publications? How critical are they to the operation of the business? *The cost: unnecessary expenditures if the information is not being used*

> During the past five years, your company has diversified at a rapid rate and you are now in several new lines of business. You have a need to stay current with these new markets and industries. The problem is that your corporate or division library does not have the depth and breadth of publications and information in these

business segments. The cost: inability to remain competitive in the marketplace

In today's complex and rapidly changing business environment, company information resources must be current, be flexible, and meet the changing environmental and business needs. The strategic information audit is not an end product and is not performed just once. It is a process that should continue to evolve. Many organizations conduct a strategic information audit or have one conducted for them on an annual basis. This process is discussed in detail later in this chapter.

The Survey

Very simply, a strategic information audit surveys the information needs of the organization, assesses how the internal information resources meet these needs, and develops a "prescription" or blueprint for a more effective corporate information or intelligence system. Depending on your corporate resources, you may have an internal group conduct the audit on its own, or have an internal group conduct the audit under the guidance of a consulting firm that specializes in this type of project.

Who should be surveyed? If possible, the strategic information audit should begin with the chief executive officer (CEO). Next, key executives, managers, and administrative staff should be interviewed at all levels of organization. Additionally, key representatives from each of the functional areas should be interviewed. Field personnel and international affiliates should also be included in the survey.

Top–Down Approach

At this point, you may be asking, How is it possible to gain support from above, namely top management? Yet, obtaining support from top management is critical to ensuring general organizational readiness for a strategic information audit. The internal champion must look toward a person in higher management who ensures top-level support for the audit. This person, who has status and political clout within the organization, will be the internal or corporate sponsor.

Top–Down Corporate Approach

A consumer packaged goods firm that employs about 10,000 people worldwide decided to conduct a full-scale information audit prior to investment in a corporate intelligence network. Approximately ninety key executives and staff at the following levels were interviewed:

- CEO (committed to the effort)
- Staff Vice-Presidents
- Functional Executive Staff
  —VP Marketing
  —VP Planning
  —Controller
  —VP Manufacturing/R&D
  —VP MIS
  —Corporate Librarians
- Divisional Staff
  —Select Product Managers
- Field/Territory Managers
- International Managers

This top–down approach ensured commitment from the CEO and senior management. Given the size of corporate expenditures on information sources and systems at every functional executive level, this approach was necessary to ensure implementation of the network. Moreover, the inclusion of field and international management minimized duplication of effort and ensured buy in from these "information rich" sources.

In this company's story, the internal champion and the internal sponsor were able to explain the rationale behind a strategic information audit, utilize influence to obtain the necessary resources, and convince top management that a strategic information audit would benefit and was consistent with the overall strategic objectives of the organization.

As in this case, the support of top management for an audit may be obtained in the following way:

- Make a presentation emphasizing the realization of cost savings that an audit can reveal, including reduced duplication of effort and less reliance on external consultants. Also emphasize the value-added elements of a shared information network and its positive impact on the organization's competitive environment (improving market share, developing new products, monitoring the competition).

- Use the influence of a corporate sponsor to obtain the necessary resources by persuading that person that the audit and resulting network will be cost efficient.

- Convince top management. Top management must be assured that a strategic information audit is consistent with the strategic objectives of the organization. Use real-life examples as to how the audit is an integral part of the shared information network and how it can improve the company's position in the marketplace. For instance, a growing number of executives have become concerned about foreign competition and the effect it has had on market share. Such an example can become the focal point of the audit and the system.

The top–down approach offers the benefit of senior management's commitment and functional and divisional management buy in to the findings of the audit. The more thorough the survey and audit, the more successful the system.

Bottom–Up Approach

Within some companies, operating divisions have very specific information needs. For instance, the research and development division of a pharmaceutical firm may have different information needs than the marketing research division of the company. For such a case, these needs are best met through a strategic information audit that focuses solely on the division, as shown in the following bottom–up approach.

Division or Bottom–Up Approach

An operating division of a bank was organized by several specific lines of business. Each line of business was unique, so the information needs and source evaluation required a separate audit. In this case, the following personnel were surveyed (thirty to thirty-five personal interviews).

- Division VP/general manager
- Division controller
- Division planner
- Division market research department
- Product managers
- Staff librarian

Because the information needs of this division were very specific, a survey was specifically designed to meet the information needs at every level of the operating division of the bank. In addition, unlike the top–down approach, this case did not require extensive support from top management or a corporatewide internal sponsor. As a result of the detailed survey and the minimizing of corporate sponsorship, this particular division was able to move quickly and transform the results of the information audit into an intelligence system.

Survey Design

Unfortunately, there is no "cookie cutter mold" for a strategic information audit survey. Even if two companies are structured similarly within the same industry, the culture of each company differs. Thus, the survey should be designed to encompass the structure of the company or division, the corporate culture, and the strategic and tactical goals of the company. Figure 4-1 is a sample questionnaire

Figure 4-1.   Basic elements of a sample questionnaire.

General Information
 1. Name, title, department
     Job description
     Factors required to perform job

Information Sources
 2. Current information sources used
     Internai sources and externally published sources
     Listing of sources (by type)
     Rating of usefulness
     Frequency of use
 3. List of documents they generate themselves
     Where are these documents located?
 4. Where do they go to find information?

Information Needs
 5. Internal document information needs (internally generated
     memos, reports, and so on)
 6. External document information needs (published materials such
     as newspapers, journals, magazines)

Communication Needs
 7. Other departments or staff needed to perform job
 8. Current method of communication internally
     (electronic mail, memo, phone)

Software/Computer Needs
 9. Do they use a personal computer, terminal, modem, hard copy?
10. Current software packages used

Wish List
11. What information sources or system would enable them
     to perform their job at optimum?
12. Describe the system

that contains the basic elements that should be covered in the interviews. A more detailed questionnaire from an actual case is discussed later in this chapter.

Questionnaires should be developed around the culture of the organization and within a planning framework. Specific questions can be tailored to specific job functions or lines of business. For instance, in the case of the research and development department of a pharmaceutical firm, one question may be, What biological or medical information sources are vital for your research and development job function? What pharmaceutical information sources? Corporate or division intelligence systems built without this initial end-user survey have little chance for success.

Who Conducts the Interviews

At this point, you may be asking, Who should conduct the interviews and analyze the results? There are two options. The first is to contract with an outside consultant. Although the company is assured objectivity and professional interviewing techniques, the consultant may lack the insight or understanding of specific lines of business or the culture of the firm. The second option is to formulate an internal task force that conducts the interviews and analyzes the results. Even though the internal staff group may know the business, the group may lack objectivity in interpreting the interviews and analyzing the results. To solve this problem, a growing number of firms are opting for a combination of having a professional firm assist an internal task force with the survey and analysis of the results. This ensures understanding of the business groups, products, and markets and also increases objectivity.

Prior to the interviewing process, the task force for interviewing staff should obtain all formal organization charts. If a combined team consists of the internal staff plus an outside consulting firm, then the internal staff should graphically draw what they believe to be the informal network so interview questions can be structured around their assumptions. This should also set the groundwork for further probing during the interviews.

How the Interviews Are Conducted

A personal oral interview is the most appropriate for a strategic information audit. Although the actual interviews are oral, the internal champion must have written documentation of all interviews. Typically, the internal champion sends letters or memos to those key personnel who are to be interviewed. The letter states the purpose of the audit and emphasizes the importance of widespread cooperation. It also notes that the person who sends the letter (internal champion or assistant) will call the interviewee to set up a mutually convenient time and place for the interview. These appointments should be set up thirty to forty-five days in advance of the interview.

Information flow can be tracked through extensive interviews (at least one hour in duration). After a series of these interviews, the informal network begins to crystallize. Each interview should consist of one or two interviewers and one interviewee.

One Company's Story

As a consultant to many Fortune 100 firms, I have either been solely responsible for designing and conducting the interviews, worked with people that I employ, or worked with the so-called internal champion of an organization. The following case documents a strategic information audit that was done for a large, vertically integrated firm.

Detailed Questionnaire
for a Vertically Integrated Company

The company is directly involved in various stages of product development. These include manufacturing, distribution, marketing, and selling. Because the firm is vertically integrated, the diverse business backgrounds of the interviewees made for a unique mix. The firm manufactures a broad array of houseware products that are prevalent in most American kitchens. In addition, the firm exploits various "cutting edge" technologies to compete in many fast-growing markets.

This case is truly unusual because it involved the efforts of two internal champions within the organization. In addition, this case was very in-depth because it considered various aspects of information flow within the firm, including the degree of satisfaction with the company's current information system, expectations of a network, current information sources, and wish lists. But most important, this particular strategic information audit was part of a phased plan, as discussed in Chapter 3, in developing a business intelligence network.

Thus, owing to the sheer size of the organization, the number of interviewees, and the detailed questionnaire (see Appendix J), such a coordinated effort was deemed necessary to bring together external objectivity and internal knowledge of the organization's diverse lines of business and competitive environment.

Note that although the company has many operating divisions that are actively involved with the information flow of the organization, the format of the questionnaire and the type of question remained the same for all those interviewed. As with other types of formalized surveys, such a format fosters consistency and increases objectivity and validity of the audit and its results.

Impact of Audit

1. The audit revealed that there was a tremendous amount of "reinventing the wheel" or duplication of efforts between the divisions of the company. A lot of the same information was being used across a number of divisions.
2. The audit also revealed that there was no investment in a corporate data base that pulled together information from a wide variety of sources.

3. The audit found that this company spent an estimated $35 million in consulting fees on an ad hoc
   basis. Approximately two-thirds of this amount was
   spent on information gathering, and the remaining
   one-third went into information analysis.
4. The audit resulted in the development of a strategic
   information data base that tracks domestic and international sources and a system that houses internal
   documents.

Bottom line estimates were that the development of a
strategic information base could save at least two-thirds of
the aforementioned consulting fees.

Developing a Strategic Intelligence Blueprint

Following the survey, the results must be synthesized and
analyzed in order to develop a strategic intelligence blueprint. Put simply, this type of blueprint is similar to one for
the construction of a house. Clearly, the survey findings
will reveal any discrepancies between the information
sources and information needs. These "holes" form the
foundation of a corporate intelligence network. For the
presentation of survey findings, a picture *is* "worth a thousand words," and senior management will respond more
effectively to a graphic presentation of the information
architecture of the company.

The information flow should also surface from the
survey, including both the formal and informal flow of
information within the company or division. Each of us is
aware of the fact that although a company or division may
publish a formal organization chart, the informal flow of
information throughout a company is what drives the business. This informal information network should be revealed
from the survey findings and be incorporated into the strategic intelligence blueprint. Such a blueprint is outlined
and charted in the following.

Discovering Information Needs

A diversified consumer packaged goods company conducted a strategic information assessment and conducted fifty-five interviews of its corporate staff. The results of the questionnaires were logged in a spreadsheet format (Table 4-1) in order to analyze the information requirements, utility of information sources, and flow of information at the corporate level.

In this case, select managers from the lines of business were also surveyed. For simplicity, we focus only on the functional areas for the blueprint.

The next step is to quantify the findings of the survey. Specifically, findings should be represented as percentages that are gleaned and analyzed. This increases the validity of the audit. The results can be quantified by applying statistical analyses to the survey answers. In this case, more than 60 percent of surveyed employees felt that the current information resources were adequate for them to conduct their job function. Moreover, the most common problems they experienced were infoglut, lack of knowledge of what other departments were doing, and lack of a structured, ongoing tracking system to keep them abreast of their business environment.

Summarizing the survey results on a grid form assisted the company in developing a blueprint of its current information architecture (Figure 4-2) and the requirements for a future information architecture that goes beyond the existing information sources.

Each functional department had a direct line of communication to the executive management committee but intermittent communication between themselves. By nature of their function, the controllers had communication with each of the functional areas. As a result, this structure lent itself to significant duplication of effort.

The strategic information audit revealed the following:

- The need for a shared information network to facilitate the flow of information between functional departments and to reduce duplication of effort

(Text continues on page 94.)

Table 4-1. Summary of responses to survey.

Functional Area	Utility of Existing Internal Documents	Info Sources External Documents	Frequency of Access	Communication Mode/Effectiveness	Information Requirements
Controllers	Plethora of data Conflicting systems	Lack of synthesized textual documents	Need daily or weekly updates	Currently by memo Need electronic system	Need access to multiple sources
Market Research	Studies in file drawers Lack of consistency	Haphazard scanning and clipping from articles	Need daily market intelligence	Currently by memo Need structured system	Need to catalog internal documents plus external intelligence
Strategic Planning	Plethora of numeric data and forecasts	Nonstructured ad hoc analysis Need global intelligence	Need monthly digest	Currently by memo or phone	Need structured approach to information for internal and external planning

Business Development	Lack of internal documents— new department	Piecemeal approach Commercial data base searches	Need corporate resource to call on for acquisition information	Currently by phone or mail	Need resource for "quick and dirty" information research requests
Research & Development	Structured library with thousands of documents Have an R&D data base but limited distribution to the rest of the company	Have extensive hard copy library of technical publications No market intelligence	Need daily access and rapid turnaround	Data base access, yet not distributed throughout the company	Need market intelligence for new product development efforts

# of personal interviews: 55
Approach: Top-down corporate staff assessment

Figure 4-2. A blueprint for corporate staff.

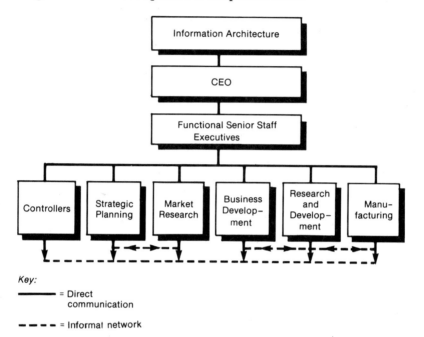

Key:

—————— = Direct
            communication

– – – – = Informal network

- The need to capture "soft" environmental and global market intelligence in a systematic manner for distribution to each of the functional areas and lines of business
- The need for an electronic mail system to facilitate interoffice communications
- The need for a corporate intelligence library

How to Track Information Flow

As previously mentioned in this chapter, the task force or interviewing staff should obtain all formal organization charts prior to the interviews. Even if the survey is being done within one line of business, obtaining such relevant information will facilitate well-structured surveys. The following company's story describes the incredible amount of information that surfaced from an interview with a product manager.

Product Manager, or Information Broker?

During an interview a product manager from a large industrial products firm stated that he considered himself an "information broker" within his business unit. When asked to explain, he outlined the situation shown in Figure 4-3.

This outline indicates that the product manager represents an information gold mine and is the nerve center of

Figure 4-3.   The product manager in relation to the information flow.

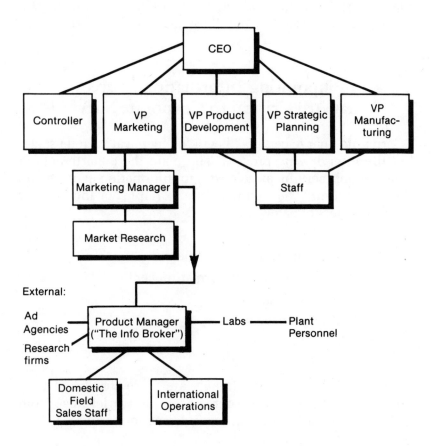

the entire organization. Logistically, he is the closest person to the external environment: ad agencies, research firms, and the company's field sales staff and plants.

When asked how he spent his time, he replied that nearly 75 to 80 percent of his time was spent on the phone disseminating what he termed "market and product intelligence." Such employees actually function as information brokers within an organization. Given his time spent on intelligence gathering and his critical position within the organization, the product manager's department was the most logical setting for a shared information network. Intelligence that is critical to the tactical and strategic operation of the firm is housed in these individuals, and a system should be developed to capture their expertise. More important, organizations experience a significant loss of intelligence or productivity when these job functions turn over.

Pinpointing Information Sources That Are Critical to Corporate Survival

Corporate "nerve centers" begin to emerge at various stages of the interviewing process. These are the departments or individuals serving as gateways to information capture and dissemination. The following are examples of intelligence nerve centers or gateways:

- Strategic planning departments
- Corporate libraries/information centers
- Technical libraries
- Product managers
- Field sales offices

Some of these departments are more structured than others, but the challenge remains to derive leverage from their investment in human and information resources.

Evaluation of the Corporate Investment in Internal and External Information Sources

Another key element that can allow an organization to assess information needs is the investment in internal and external information sources. By this, I mean: What does it cost an organization to attain, gather, store, and disseminate information that is obtained either within the organization or from external and published sources?

Investment in Internal Information Sources

Investment in internal information sources can be enormous. Corporate executives do not realize the tremendous investment that they have made in these sources. Internal information sources can be defined simply as those documents created on a daily basis by employees of the company. Despite this simple definition, the dollar investment in terms of generation, dissemination, and storage of these documents is staggering.

To tackle this issue, an organization should focus on a single department. The following simple equation can be applied to derive the corporate investment in internal documents:

$$\text{Corporate Investment in Internal Documents} =$$

$$\frac{\text{Number of Hours to}}{\text{Generate Document}} \times \frac{\text{Labor}}{\text{Rate(s)}} +$$

$$\frac{\text{Cost of Input to}}{\text{Develop the Document}} + \frac{\text{Cost of Document}}{\text{Materials}}$$

For example, a document generated by the research and development department is valued at the total hours to draft the document (at the hourly rate of the drafter and administrative staff) plus the cost of research (which is defined as input to develop the document) plus the cost of materials of the document. Clearly, documents generated at high labor rates and high cost of input (research and development, strategic planning, marketing research departments) carry a high corporate investment. If an executive were to calculate the corporate investment in these documents, the amount would be exorbitant. Additionally, these numbers should also be weighed according to their strategic impact on the corporation, such as a technological breakthrough (for example, the development of Olestra, a new fat substitute from Procter & Gamble).

Investment in External Information

Although investment cost in external information may be more tangible than the cost of internal information, the numbers are even more staggering. External information consists of those documents that have been purchased by the company in its normal course of conducting business. The following are examples of these documents:

- Newspapers
- Publications (journals, newsletters)
- Books
- Management consulting studies
- Market research studies
- Legal library documents
- Technical library documents (software documents)
- Reference materials
- Videotapes
- Training materials
- Speeches
- Material from conferences and trade shows

To derive the corporate investment in external documents, the following formula can be applied:

$$\text{Corporate Investment in External Documents} =$$

$$\text{Actual Cost of the Document} + \text{Manager's Time to Digest Document} +$$

$$\text{Cost to Distribute Document} + \text{Cost to Store Document}$$

To summarize, the cost of "corporate intelligence" is the sum of the company's investment in its internal and external documents. It should be clear that the inability to gain rapid access to these documents translates into a significant loss for the corporation.

Application to Small Business

Most of this chapter sounds very "upscale." What if your company has a small functional staff (marketing/sales, controller, and research)? Although your firm may appear to have more of an informal than a formal network, you should not ignore the exercise of a strategic information assessment and blueprint for your organization.

Clearly, small businesses have tangible advantages over large organizations in that they can conduct a strategic information audit in less time and with greater chance of cooperation from colleagues. Typically, for a firm that has annual sales of $100 million with one hundred employees, the audit may consist of as few as twenty-five to thirty interviews. For a firm with annual sales of $10 million with fifty employees, the number of interviews may be a dozen or so.

If your organization does not have many layers of staff, consider assigning a qualified member (for example, the controller) to conduct the audit. If your firm is growing, the audit should be updated as you add staff and functional areas. In short, you are in a prime position to assess your information needs early.

Summary

Whether your organization is a Fortune 500 firm or a five-year-old startup, the strategic information audit can prove to be a powerful determinant in assessing information needs. In addition, the various aspects of the audit can actually result in proactive decision making, such as in determining how much to invest in information sources.

5

Internal Information Sources

"Information may be accumulated in files, but it must be retrieved to be of use in decision making."

Kenneth J. Arrow, Nobel laureate in economics

Internal information sources are those documents generated by internal staff. Many organizations suffer from an overload of such paperwork. Although a large portion of internal information may not be valuable to many employees in an organization, 10 to 20 percent of it is vital to the corporate operation. How can a company sift through this mass of information and identify, store, and disseminate the critical portion? In this chapter we delineate a process for data capture.

How often have you been at a meeting and wanted to refer to a document that discussed similar issues months before? Or take the situation where you were assigned to conduct a study to evaluate a new market. After two months, your department had spent hundreds of hours on the project only to discover that another department had conducted a similar project six months before. Had you known of the prior study, you could have saved hundreds if not thousands of dollars by not "reinventing the wheel." Clearly, the cataloguing of relevant internally generated documents translates into dollars and cents for corporations.

On the other hand, some internal reports are generally distributed to a small group of employees on a "need to know" basis. Unless the results of the studies are understood to be crucial, a vast number of employees do not have access to this information, and are cut out of the intelligence loop. As a result, executives in planning, marketing, and financial positions are developing corporate strategies, marketing plans, and acquisition or divestiture plans with less than optimum information. It is amazing to discover how much of this valuable or strategic information is housed internally.

Internal documents generated by organizations can be classified as follows:

- Internally generated operational memoranda
  —Daily, weekly, monthly, quarterly reports
  —Production reports, sales reports, financial reports
- Internally generated analytical reports
  —Marketing reports, strategic planning documents
  —Management science reports, economic reports, newsletters
- Purchased reports from external vendors
  —Market research reports
  —Advertising studies
  —Published reports from consulting firms
- Internally generated clippings and documents
  —Clippings from the print media
  —Documents from the corporate library
  —Documents from corporate communications or public relations

Operational Memoranda

Operational memoranda include memos, reports, and status documents generated on either a systematic or an ad hoc basis. Such sources may entail the systematic tracking of internal operations by updating employees as to the status of a new product, marketing activities, or financial data. To give an example, the regional sales manager of the frozen

foods division of a large packaged foods manufacturer distributes a two-page status report to division management.
The report highlights consumers' initial reactions to a new
frozen entrée that is being test marketed in the Southeast.
In paraphrased form, it might look like this:

Status Report
Frozen Food Sales—Southeast Region

Supermarket managers in Atlanta and Florida have told
us that consumers have reacted favorably to our new
frozen entrée. One Piggly Wiggly outlet in Orlando
noted that thirty-day supplies of the product were sold
out in two and one-half weeks.

Retailers tell us that the product is priced just right
and that their expectations have been met. Thus, it
appears that our goal of attaining 11 percent margins
for frozen foods will be achieved. In addition, the
prospects for a successful national rollout of the entrée
are excellent.

Such general, yet vital internal information sources are
most closely associated with the day-to-day operations of
an organization.

Analytical Reports

Analytical reports can be defined as internal sources that
analyze developments within the organization or its business environment. Generally, these sources are used to
provide insights into the future direction of the organization
or information about its competitive environment. Compared with operational memoranda, analytical reports differ
in that they are usually written by or distributed to senior-
level executives.

To give an example, the strategic planning division of a
large investment firm proposed to senior management to
produce an internal report that would analyze the company's unprofitable discount brokerage unit. A section of the
"executive summary" may look something like this:

Executive Summary
XYZ Discount Brokerage Unit

The purpose of this report is to provide senior management with a foundation document regarding the company's XYZ discount brokerage unit. The report analyzes the unit's history and operations and makes several recommendations as to the future of the unit.

Various factors, including the stock market crash of 1987 and a drastic reduction of individual investors in the market, may necessitate a cost-cutting strategy for this unit. Future plans may call for a divestment of the discount brokerage unit.

As this example illustrates, analytical reports tend to be actionable and future-oriented sources of internal information.

Consultants' Reports

In addition to gathering information from staff, many companies look to external suppliers of information. Oftentimes, a company contracts with an advertising agency, a marketing research firm, or a consulting firm to provide a study on a given topic. Most of these studies, although derived from an external supplier, are used solely for the internal purposes of the organization. In most cases, the external information supplier signs some sort of exclusivity agreement with the organization.

Internal Clippings and Documents

Internally generated clippings and documents are usually housed in an information center or corporate library. They include such documents as clippings from published sources, business periodicals, organizational procedures and guidelines, and manuals. They may also include internally published information that profiles or highlights key events that affect the organization. Many corporations have set up communications or public relations departments, which are also settings for this type of internal information.

The Investment

As a corporation grows in size, it is virtually impossible for every department head or manager to be aware of all of the internal correspondence generated within the department, much less the entire firm. As such, an ongoing procedure must be established to provide for selection of those documents to be placed either in hard copy files or in electronic data base format. The following case shows the investment versus value-added ratio of documents. The document utility evaluation (Table 5-1) can actually screen the value and utility of internal documents.

To Toss or Not to Toss

A large financial institution commissioned my firm to screen thousands of internally generated documents for input to a sophisticated and widely distributed system. During the strategic information audit (discussed in Chapter 4), I conducted an extensive evaluation of the company's internally generated documents. Rather than cataloguing and inputting a summary of every document, I developed criteria for the selection of material. I then developed a grid form (Table 5-1) that quantified the utility of the documents to the department and the total organization. Using a scale of 0.00–1.00, I factored the value and reusability of each document and retained those having average values of 3.75 or higher. Department management estimated the ratings because they were better qualified to estimate the utility of the document.

In this case, the archival value of several documents (such as old planning documents and market research reports) was high. However, the impact on the current and future business was low. Moreover, it was unlikely that more than ten users would access these documents within the life span of the data base or hard copy library. On the other hand, a document may have only moderate or low impact on the business, yet the cost of duplicating the effort or "reinventing the wheel" may be high enough to merit archiving the document.

Table 5-1. Document utility evaluation.

Date of Publication	Archival Value of Content	Estimated Number of Users	Impact on the Business	Cost of Duplication	Total Rating	Suggested Action
1.00 = 1 year old	1.00 = high	1.00 = 50	1.00 = high	1.00 = $10,000	5.00	input document
0.75 = 2–4 years old	0.75 = med.	0.75 = 25	0.75 = mod.	0.75 = $ 5,000	3.75	input document
0.50 = 5 + years old	0.50 = low	0.50 = <10	0.50 = low	0.50 = $ 500	2.50	toss document

Two thousand documents from each department were audited. Out of this total, approximately 60 percent, or 1,200, were defined as having "strategic value" or utility to the organization. I recommended to management that they toss the remaining documents. Should they need to be archived for legal reasons, they are probably best archived in an off-site facility.

This audit and the decision to toss or not toss not only assisted department management with records management but also forced them to think strategically about their investment in internal information. For example, say a study was ten years old and contained consumers' attitudes toward automated teller machines (ATMs) in the Southwest. Management had to ask themselves the question, Given the current proliferation of ATMs, of what value is this report?

They also had to analyze the value of the content of the report, which indicated considerable initial consumer resistance to the technology. In introducing new technology-based products, will the bank find consumer resistance equally prevalent in the Southwest? Here, the document could have low archival value to the organization but high impact on the business if the financial institution were launching new technology-based consumer products and selecting possible test markets.

Given the archival value and high-impact potential of the report, management decided to keep it. In addition, it was determined that such a report could cause management to rethink its current strategy, especially because technology developments have broad-based implications for the financial services industry. The department found the grid valuable in reaching that decision.

After criteria for retaining documents were set up, the next step was for the department to maintain this system on an ongoing basis. Thus, the first process was to teach the "to toss or not to toss" process by determining the value of internal documents to the department. In one case, the department consisted of a librarian and a supervisor. After internal staff were indoctrinated for one week (included in the indoctrination was the development and documentation of the system), it was decided that they would conduct this audit on an annual basis. This annual review streamlined the process while not creating an overabundance of documents to audit. It took about one to two weeks a year to perform this audit, which became an integral updating process within the department.

How to Digest and Catalog Internal Information Sources

Regardless of whether a firm decides to launch this process by itself or decides to seek expert help, the need exists for digesting and cataloging internal documents. Whether the firm is a one-million-dollar company or a multibillion-dollar firm, this task should not be ignored.

The cataloging process should be kept simple for both large and small firms. If you cannot fit it on one page or on one computer screen, it is probably not worth "reprocessing" the information. Both internal and external labor are expensive, and the cost of developing these systems (even if they are in hard copy) should not exceed their value.

Citibank Climbs out of the Box

A department of Citibank approached us with a large number of diverse documents to be catalogued. The challenge was to develop a standard format that would allow us to input documents from internal reports, memoranda, field studies, clippings, advertisements, and planning documents. It was also imperative to be able to retrieve the document from one of several hard copy libraries within the institution. Moreover, it was the vision of senior management to have this data base in electronic format and as part of a larger system that integrated internal information with external information.

Following an extensive utility audit, I focused on designing a one-page intelligence screen for the documents selected to be put into the system. Because internal documents are bibliographic in nature, the following screen design was selected:

Document # (to be used to access the document in the hard copy library):

Title:

Author:

Department:

Subject:

Key Findings:

Key Words:

Each document was assigned a number that matched the physical library number for retrieval. Key words were also added to each screen citation to enable the document to be found. In addition, this data base was written in a straightforward textual format that ensured that the documents could be transported from system to system, regardless of the software or hardware requirements.

Structure of the System. As we developed the data base, we entered it on a personal computer that used a text retrieval package. This allowed end users within the bank to "play" with the package and evaluate the contents of the data base. Following the development of a prototype, it was clear that the bank wanted to distribute the information to a wide range of users throughout the bank. Because our flat files were not tied to any hardware or software, we were able to transport them to a mainframe system for access by several hundred users via personal computers (see Figure 5-1).

Ongoing Maintenance of the System. To ensure continued upkeep of the system, we trained the internal staff in document analysis skills and data base development procedures. On the citations, the bank has tagged certain documents as a "must read," which describes the impact or importance of the document.

Benefits of the System. Several hundred users in this bank are now able to access updates of internal documents on an ongoing basis. Reports that were once piled up on employees' desks are now placed in a system that alerts employees who should read them. In such a case, the system has a feature that acts as a trigger to alert employees

Figure 5-1. Citibank's system for access to internal documents.

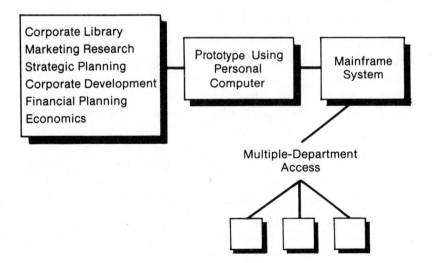

to new information, such as a telephone hot line, internal memoranda from the department, or a computerized network or electronic mail system. Another benefit is that the users have access to scanned, synthesized information from the external environment that is all pulled together in one system. This one-stop-shopping approach has enabled the bank to deal with the issue of information overload.

According to Citibank, "The financial industry demands speed, but a big company moves slowly, partly because it is paralyzed by not knowing what to do with the reams of information it has access to." Having a synthesized digest of internal documents at their fingertips enables management to quickly respond to market conditions or, more important, develop a proactive strategy vis-à-vis their competitors.[1]

Other Ways to Synthesize and Store Internal Documents

There are other means of synthesizing and storing internal documents. In most instances, the ways and means depend on the structure, size, and resources of the organization.

Efficient Systems Using Personal Computers

What about marketing research departments that are swamped with focus-group studies, field surveys, syndicated studies, product reports, advertising effectiveness reports, ad infinitum? Although the need may not exist for the entire organization to have access to the information, the need does exist for cataloging these internal documents.

Executives such as Jim Figura, corporate director of worldwide marketing services, Colgate-Palmolive, recognized this need several years ago. With the large amount of documents generated within the market research function,

---

[1]"A Tale of Two Companies Coping With Information Overload." Reprinted from PC Week, June 21, 1988, pp. 59, 64. Copyright © 1988 Ziff Communications Company.

he visualized a corporate library system that provided for the systematic organization of internal documents. During the past few years, Colgate-Palmolive has developed a series of internal data bases that catalog strategic documents. These internal documents, which are strictly confidential to Colgate-Palmolive, are categorized by the company's existing lines of business, new ventures, possible future lines of business, and geographic areas of interest. The documents are also efficiently managed on personal computers.

As a result of this in-depth coverage, the corporate marketing function is able to manage, on a worldwide basis, the flow of market and product-category information between operating subsidiaries.

Efficient Hard Copy Systems

What if you are employed by a smaller company not yet glutted with internal documents because the company is spending most of its time either building or putting out operational fires? You can begin developing a system now by putting together a hard copy file structure that will allow you to automate the system at a later time. Do not wait until your firm reaches $5 million, $10 million, or $20 million in revenues and you are faced with information overload and the inability to react quickly. The company story that follows profiles a small consulting firm that eventually outgrew its hard copy library.

Converting From a Hard Copy to an Electronic System

A small consulting firm had a very skilled librarian, who by nature of her training had developed a one-page, hard copy summary of each document in its files. As the firm grew, she continued to catalog the reports by subject, title, and author, in addition to adding a brief summary of the project. When the firm automated several of its functions, the library files were in excellent shape for data entry specialists to type in their summaries for the development of their project data base. Had this hard copy system not been developed from the inception of the firm, the firm would have been faced with digesting more than 30,000 documents for entry into the data base. Clearly, this would have cost thousands of dollars in terms of internal effort or with the assistance of an outside firm. At this point, it was much easier to load in 30,000 one-sheet document summaries than to abstract that many documents.

Do It Yourself Versus Hire Suppliers

Suppose your firm has decided to tackle its information overload problem in terms of internal documents. You have recently formed a committee to execute this task. You are now faced with the following issues:

- Does our firm have the resources or experience to design this type of data base?
- Who will analyze and catalog the documents?
- Who will summarize and index the documents?
- Can our internal information systems staff evaluate the hardware and software requirements?
- How do we prototype or test the system?

Information systems are skill- and labor-intensive systems. It takes approximately eight or nine skilled document analysts to input between 1,200 and 1,500 documents during a six-week prototype period. Large firms should conduct internal cost analysis to determine whether to make or to buy.

Smaller firms that want to develop a cataloging system for their internal documents (before the situation gets out of hand) should consider committing an administrative person to either catalog the internal documents in handwritten form or enter the data on a simple personal computer data base package. As the company grows, these files can be transferred to the corporate intelligence data base.

Hardware and Software Issues

Regarding the design and building of strategic intelligence systems, I have only three words of wisdom: flexibility, flexibility, and more flexibility.

Intelligence systems are end user based and should be custom-designed. Even within the same industry, no two companies view their industry, their market, their competition in the same manner.

For example, my firm developed an automotive competitive intelligence data base ("AUTO"), which is an off-the-shelf monitoring service of competitive activity within the automotive industry. During a trip to Detroit to sell subscriptions to the data base, I met with the "Big Three" auto producers. I displayed the same abstracts to all three automakers, and I received three entirely different views on the information. In my experience with the development of intelligence systems over the past six years, no two direct competitors in the same industry and the same markets view information in the same way. This is a powerful message for computer and software producers. The corporate end user wants a custom-designed intelligence network, despite the fact that the company may use industry software and hardware products.

During my tenure as a senior planning manager within an information systems group for a large confectionery company, I quickly realized that decision support systems could only go so far in terms of building strategic intelligence systems. These systems require text retrieval along with graphics capabilities and, perhaps, access to precalculated numeric data. In our effort to design and develop these systems, we experimented with several text retrieval packages, executive information systems, and relational data base management packages.

We found no package with a solution for the integration of text and numeric information. The good news, however, is that these packages can be custom-designed for corporate intelligence applications. Two driving factors for the selection of the hardware and software for these systems are (1) the culture of the company and (2) the results of the strategic information audit.

The data bases should be set up in a simple computerized textual format to ensure transferability of the files as hardware and software technologies change. This will make the files readable by various operating systems and software packages. The format decision should also depend on whether your system will be exclusively for use by one department or will be distributed throughout the entire company. Clearly, personal computer systems are better suited for the former applications, and mainframe systems are a necessity for the latter.

Legal and Copyright Issues

Documents written internally by employees are generally the exclusive property of the company. These documents may include internally generated operational memoranda and internally generated analytical reports. In most cases, firms can input a summary or even full text of the documents in an electronic format without any problem.

However, documents purchased by the company but written by an outside firm that holds copyright to them are another issue. These documents cannot be duplicated or input electronically without the permission of the publisher. As in a traditional card catalog system, you can catalog the subject, title, author, date of publication, and location of the document for reference purposes. If you are considering inputting a brief summary or analysis of the document, you should contact the publisher to obtain permission to do so. Because publishers are entitled to royalty payments for duplication of their work, you are always safer to contact your internal legal staff or publisher first.

Cost Savings

Corporations have made an enormous investment in internal information, which is rarely quantified. Use this simple formula to calculate the cost of your investment in internal documents.

$$\frac{\text{Cost of}}{\text{Document}} = \frac{\text{Number of Manpower Hours}}{\text{to Generate Document}} \times$$

$$\frac{\text{Labor}}{\text{Rate}} = \frac{\text{Value of Document}}{\text{Storage}}$$

Example: New Product Development Project

5 professionals/1,000 hours each or 5,000 hours ×
$25/hour = $125,000 spent on producing the document

Impact of document: potential $10 million new product
line

Duplication of effort factor: at least $62,500 (50% of
total cost)

Loss of intelligence factor (lack of distribution of information): estimated at $50,000

Cost of document input and storage: $15–$25/docu-
ment (either in hard copy, electronic, or CD-ROM
format)

Net result: The advantages of inputting this document
clearly outweigh the cost of duplication of effort for
the report or the loss of intelligence by other marketing, sales, or financial staff not knowing the potential
of this $10 million new product line.

Summary

Companies with their internal documents "at their fingertips" will clearly have a competitive edge during the next
decade. As information systems are built on a global basis,
corporations will increase their strategic intelligence and
their ability to react quickly to changing business conditions.

6

External Information Sources

"The power of external information can be extremely useful in energizing new product development efforts. By systematically gathering information on competitive activity, good ideas can be easily spotted and development time dramatically shortened."

Tim Armour, Vice-President, Citibank

Although executives use various internal information sources, their decision making is largely based on several years of industry experience and external information sources. External information sources consist of information or intelligence that is generated outside the organization and is made available on an industrywide basis or to the general public. This chapter focuses on external information sources as they apply to a shared information network.

As corporations continue to eliminate many layers of management and as the job descriptions of today's managers become more complex, it is nearly impossible for many executives and managers to keep abreast of all the relevant external information sources in their field. Most of this information is found in newspapers, publications, conferences, speeches, trade shows, and so on. As opposed to internally published information sources that are distributed only within the organization, external information sources contain information that is available to anyone who wants it. In addition, external information sources are more tactical in scope, whereas internal sources have a more strategic scope. That is, information derived outside an organization is usually only information that the publisher wants to be made public or information that the media is able to attain. Because the number of external information sources is enormous, business professionals at all levels are faced with the challenge of what to do with all this information.

Incorporating external information sources into a shared information network is a major problem. Many corporations encounter difficulties in filtering through external information sources and organizing the information as it pertains to the competitive business environments of the organization. Many corporations are faced with a structural problem in gathering external information sources. For instance, a company that has many layers of management is more likely to experience difficulties in effectively gathering and organizing information from external sources.

The solution involves the development of a structured process that tracks and monitors external information sources, captures news and events relevant to the organization, and distributes this information in an effective manner. Such a process can be executed either internally or by an external organization that has the resources and the expertise in information management. A major objective of this solution is that information derived from external sources must be made available to the organization on a timely basis and be customized to the specific needs of the business manager.

Executives need to have external information that parallels the strategic objectives of the organization, its competitors (present and potential), its markets (present and potential), and its products and services (present and potential). Many American corporations are so inner-focused. That is, corporate executives and managers spend an inordinate amount of time keeping abreast of the internal operations and performance of their organization. In addition, management has also become very dependent on information generated internally, so much so that it often misses "soft information" that affects the industry and marketplace.

Soft Information

Unlike most internal information sources that contain data for the eyes of the organization only (for example, actual results of a test market for a new product), soft information is largely in textual format (books, periodicals, radio and television, advertisements). The importance of soft information should not be underestimated. A growing part of executive decision making is based on reactions from soft information. Examples of soft information include:

- Newspapers
- Periodicals
- Books
- Advertisements
- Television
- Radio announcements
- Newsletters
- Government reports
- Legal documents
- Conference proceedings
- Commercial data bases
- Press conferences and press releases
- Company annual reports and quarterly reports

These soft information sources can have profound effects, either positive or negative, on business decisions.

Newspapers

Because newspapers are probably the information source most closely associated with a general audience, they frequently affect business decisions. In one such case, the department manager of a bank cited a summarized article from a shared information network in his department. The summary, which was referenced from a trade newspaper, pertained to a new direct payroll deposit program that a branch of the federal government wanted to set up. In reacting to this citation, the bank manager printed the summary and reference and brought it to the attention of his colleagues. Within a week, the department of the bank organized a task force, developed a proposal for this branch of the government, and flew to Washington, D.C., to make a presentation. As it turned out, the bank won this contract, which was worth millions of dollars.

Incidentally, the bank manager found this article about two weeks after it had been published. Even though the bank had about 12,000 subscriptions to this particular publication, it took a shared information network to turn what appeared to be passive information into active information.

Periodicals

Magazines and other periodicals that pertain to a particular industry have become vital in monitoring new developments in the industry and in tracking competition. For instance, when a representative of a major food manufacturer was shown an article from a periodical about a new product called Pasta Pops, which are actually frozen pasta pops on a stick, his first reaction was laughter. However, after he distributed this article to various departments, including the company's new business development department, the feedback he got was that the article represented a missed new product development opportunity.

Advertisements

Advertisements and conferences are soft information sources that reveal subtle, yet important information about competitive activity and new products and services that can affect business decisions.

Many corporations run advertisements in trade publications to promote new products or offer new services to customers. Such advertisements can give insights into the direction of a company and are especially useful in monitoring the competition. For instance, if a manufacturer of frozen entrées runs an advertisement in a supermarket trade publication that touts its brand of frozen entrées, yet does not mention or graphically depict the entrée in the ad, the competition can infer that the company will look to extend its brand name to other food categories. Thus, the competition may know what the frozen food manufacturer is doing even before it does it and make proactive decisions on the basis of the advertisement.

Books and Government Reports

Books and government reports can be important external information sources that are high in utility. Oftentimes, these sources provide vital statistics or data on a particular business, market, or company. Over the years, various business-related textbooks have become more and more prevalent in American corporations. One example is the highly acclaimed *The Renewal Factor*, by Bob Waterman.

Various branches within the federal government publish reports, either periodically or on a systematic basis, that track business-related topics. For instance, the Commerce Department monitors various economic factors that affect U.S. business activity. These factors include gross national product, inflation rates, employment and unemployment data, and many others. These data are compiled by many organizations and have become key economic indicators for the financial community.

Company Annual Reports

Company annual reports are publications that are internally generated yet made available to company shareholders, libraries, and oftentimes the general public. Many people refer to annual reports for financial information and to track a particular company over time. However, much of the information in annual reports is "puffery" that focuses on how "well" an organization is performing. In addition, annual reports do not offer insights as to strategy and future direction, and because they are published annually, they are not timely documents. Thus, annual reports are examples of soft information sources that, although useful in some instances (for example, financial information), do not have a high degree of utility.

Categorizing External Information Sources

It is easy to become overwhelmed by the amount of external information necessary to keep executives and managers abreast of their business and competitive environments. The number of commercial on-line data base providers that track and summarize soft information has increased at a rapid rate during the past decade. Although many do a good job of categorizing information from various sources, most data base publishers and distributors offer a "supermarket" approach to the access of external information sources. That is, many of these services are "generic" and are not customized or tailored toward the information requirements of corporations. Thus, although commercial data bases can be used effectively and can be useful to businesspeople in many instances, they do not provide business intelligence and analysis.

There are instances when commercial data bases can be used effectively for information gathering. They are effective when used to find current or historical information on a particular subject. Because many commercial data bases cost as much as $150 an hour to tap into, they must be searched in an economical way. For instance, many data bases allow users to search within a particular time frame. This can be very helpful because it allows those seeking information on a particular subject to do so on a systematic basis.

More and more American corporations are interested in monitoring business developments in the Far East. Because there is a language barrier, however, it has become difficult for some organizations to track such international information. As a result, some organizations have developed commercial data bases that translate Japanese and other Asian publications into English.

Commercial data bases can assist businesspeople in finding information in areas they do not have expertise in. For instance, there are data bases that offer high-technology or research-intensive information not usually available as soft information, such as medical, pharmaceutical, and chemical research findings.

Monitoring External Information

Although companies often need to look at a specific company or product, executives need to be aware of their industry and environment on a constant basis. It is useful to monitor external information sources in the following sequence:

1. The industry
2. The market
3. Companies
4. Products
5. Specific topics

This way, the executive can view the overall emerging trends within a particular industry. The executive can also monitor other industries that affect his. Many call this the fading of lines between industries. For instance, during the early 1980s, deregulation of the financial services industry was a major factor that caused a fading of lines between traditional commercial banks, securities firms, insurance firms, and nonbanks. Thus, for retirement savings products in the financial services industry, the procedure for tracking external information sources would look something like Table 6-1.

The notion of fading lines between industries leads us to the next consideration, why it is imperative for business professionals to take a strategic view of their industry, markets, and products through "cross-industry impact analysis."

Cross-Industry Impact Analysis

Soft information about a particular industry may have broad implications for other industries. This is what is meant by cross-industry impact analysis, a concept that can be ap-

Table 6-1. Monitoring external information sources in the financial services industry.

The Industry	The Market	Companies	Products	Specific Topics
Financial services	Retirement savings plans	Banks Thrifts Insurance Securities Nonbanks	Individual retirement accounts Keogh plans 401(k) plans Mutual funds	Demographics Life-styles Delivery/ distribution Industry/issues Legislation/ regulation New products Economic trends

plied to information management. Just think of the following situation:

> A consumer (CONSUMER) brushes his teeth in the morning, drives a car (AUTO) to work, uses an automatic teller machine at the bank at noon (ATM/FINANCIAL SERVICES), returns to the office and uses a personal computer (TECHNOLOGY), picks up a prescription (PHARMACEUTICALS/HEALTH CARE) on the way home, goes home and prepares dinner (FOOD), and calls his parents (MATURING CONSUMER/LIFE-STYLES, DEMOGRAPHICS) in the evening.

This scenario underscores the fact that many corporations only track and monitor industries that they are actively involved with. In addition, although many corporations view consumer buying behavior within their respective industries and markets, they sometimes do not take the interrelationships between industries into consideration. In short, companies must monitor their macroenvironment, not just their microenvironment.

Electronic components will account for as much as 35 percent of the total components of the typical automobile during the 1990s. Taking this into consideration, some corporations that market computers, software, and electronic gadgetry are actively monitoring developments and competitors in the automotive industry. In addition, some of these companies, which historically have been most closely associated with offering computers and systems to large organizations, are also tracking developments among component suppliers to the automotive industry. This example underscores how some computer, software, and electronic manufacturers are viewing their microenvironments and incorporating cross-industry impact analysis.

The key to this example is that these select companies have broadly defined their strategic focus. If a company sells products to consumers, how can its employees possibly read all the external literature that relates to consumers' lives on a daily basis, much less track domestic and global competitors' strategies with the enormous amount of external information available? Clearly, the company has to define a strategic focus. Someone (or several people) in the organization has to select those publications that need to be scanned on an ongoing basis and synthesize the material for input into a network or system, which can be accessed by key executives.

This person or group of people consists of the internal champion and the task force responsible for setting up the network. This group should develop an external information source list according to the strategic objectives of the organization, its competitors and lines of business, existing cross-industry impact analyses, and potential new analyses. In many corporations, this list of external sources is quite extensive.

Do External Information Sources Meet Strategic Objectives?

Most companies subscribe to industry trade publications in addition to general business publications and newspapers. In spite of the demands on their time, most executives attempt to stay current about their industry, markets, competitors, and products. Even though most executives do a good job of staying aware of the key issues facing their business, it is not humanly possible to be aware of every current event that could affect an industry. Thus, a structured approach is necessary to ensure that this data or intelligence is captured.

In establishing this process, the first step is to evaluate the information sources to which your company currently subscribes. The following questions must then be asked:

1. *Are these publications too narrow in focus?* For instance, some publications, although relevant to a particular industry, are too technical in scope. Others cover tangential industries. In such cases, it may be best not to subscribe to the publications but rather to use commercial data bases to access such information on an as-needed basis.

2. *Do they include information on only current competitors, rather than potential competitors?* A yes to this question may indicate the need for the internal champion or the task force to develop a list of direct competitors, a list of indirect competitors, and a list of potential competitors. This would allow the group to effectively evaluate each one listed, refine the list, and make publication choices from a finalized list of competitors.

3. *Do they only cover domestic competitors and markets?* Nowadays, this has become a vital question because more and more corporations are interested in monitoring overseas information. Thus, for many organizations that have interests overseas or are looking to enter new markets overseas, publications that cover only domestic competitors and markets will not suffice.

4. *Who has access to these publications?* Answering this question may involve the process of assessing the internal demand for each publication. This can be done in either a structured or unstructured manner.

5. *What is the time lag from receipt of publication to your reading the publication?* Because many external information sources are sometimes distributed to key executives well after the organization receives them (sometimes two to

three weeks), this question is important to answer, for it can give the task force an idea of how often the shared information network should be updated.

6. *What is the procedure if an employee notes a key article? Is the article circulated? If so, who is on the circulation list?* This question is critical because it can give the task force insights into the internal practices of publication distribution and lay the groundwork for the distribution of the shared information network.

7. *Do information gatekeepers exist within the organization? If so, do they accelerate or block the dissemination of information?* This question relates to the hoarding and infoglut factors. Clearly, information gatekeepers can promote or impede information dissemination.

Answering these questions is the first step in developing a structured process that gathers and synthesizes information from external sources on an ongoing basis. In addition, the information that is gathered and synthesized should be incorporated into a shared information network. According to Jim Onalfo, desserts division systems manager for General Foods Corporation, "If the information is not structured, many people may not see it. Or, if they see it, they may not understand the essential message. You've got to point people to the information they should be reading, and that's what a strategic intelligence data base does."

Clearly, a method must be in place to process this information. This is a very labor-intensive process and it is up to the corporation to determine if it is more economical to contract with an external firm, allocate internal resources to develop the process, or use a combination of both. General Foods found it more economical to use an outside service for gathering and synthesizing external information sources. According to Onalfo, "I had developed a very ambitious strategic information plan three years earlier [in 1984] and had accomplished all platforms of it, except installing an information-delivery tool detailing the activities of the competition."

Onalfo found that this was far too expensive to do

internally because the division would have to hire a person with extremely sophisticated information-scanning skills. Additionally, he estimated that he would have to subscribe to a huge number of journals and data bases and train the staffer to scan, synthesize, and digest exactly what was needed. What was needed was not only a service to scan, synthesize, and digest the information, but also a data base and distribution mechanism to provide structure for the information.

At General Foods, a text search system was developed that enabled employees to download from the data base summaries from prechosen articles and reports scanned by researchers at an outside firm. Approximately forty dessert-sector employees are using the system regularly. The information they are accessing answers the question, What is the competition doing that General Foods should know about? According to Onalfo, General Foods would not be spending upward of $50,000 annually on this system if it did not represent increased revenues.

General Foods is a multinational food company with interests in many markets and products. Clearly, in a small company the best way to track and monitor external information sources is to build hard copy files that store the information. As the firm grows, this information can be integrated into a cost-efficient personal computer system. The following company's story discusses how an advertising agency developed such a system.

A Growing Firm Expands Its Information Tracking and Storing

A small advertising firm (annual billings of $40 million) did not have the resources to develop a research department. The agency began to subscribe to various journals in the industries it was servicing. As its business increased in certain market sectors, it employed a librarian who scanned and clipped key articles of interest and put them into hard copy file folders.

However, within a couple of years and largely owing to

changes in the industries that the agency serviced, these files became fragmented and difficult to manage. The agency serves the personal care, food, and health care industries and the lines between some of the markets within these industries were fading. For instance, companies that marketed personal care products (for example, deodorant) entered the health care industry and vice versa. Thus, it became difficult to determine what articles belonged in which file folders.

The firm decided to employ a few research professionals to keep abreast of its clients' industries. These professionals scanned, clipped, and analyzed external information sources that related to the industries of interest. In addition, they wrote reports and made presentations to senior management on the basis of this soft information and its inferences.

The existing information network, which had been set up years prior and used a mainframe computer, did not monitor and track external information sources and was largely based on the internal operations of the agency.

As the ad agency realized that it was necessary to monitor external information sources on a systematic basis, the research staff and company librarian, with the assistance of an outside firm, developed a series of data bases that provided this information to the account executives. These data bases summarized relevant information according to a predetermined list of external information sources, including newspapers, periodicals and trade publications, press releases, and other forms of soft information published on a timely basis.

These data bases provided cross-industry impact analysis and they were customized to the needs of the firm. This subset of an existing shared information network became an integral part of the agency's networking environment. As the agency grew in size and won new accounts, the decision was made to hire an outside firm. This allowed the agency to concentrate its efforts internally on using the intelligence for successful advertising campaigns.

Summary

An organization that has timely and continued access to external information sources, in addition to internal documents, can gain an advantage vis-à-vis its competitors. The next step is to effectively integrate these two types of information sources into a shared information network, which is discussed in the next chapter.

7

Building the System

"There is no substitute for User contact. Ford's online Corporate Technical Information System relied on direction from probable Users during development for both content and system design. We have gone back three times for expansion guidance. CTIS is User driven . . . note the capital U."

F. C. Linder, Engineering and Manufacturing Staff,
Ford Motor Company

A shared information network is an excellent way for organizations to systematically monitor their industry, markets, products, and competitors. However, there are some issues and critical success factors that are involved. This chapter focuses on the structural aspects of a shared information network (for example, the data base design), the technical aspects of a shared information network (such as software and hardware requirements), the "integrity" issues involved in maintaining the system, and the costs associated with the network.

Shared information or intelligence systems should reflect how management "views" the industry, markets, products, and competitors. To incorporate this thinking into the design of a shared information network and to provide other success factors, input must be obtained from key strategic planning, marketing, sales, financial, and manufacturing executives.

Data Base Design

Data bases sound very technical and are quite intimidating to most business executives. They should be designed around the strategic objectives of an organization. The data base designer should draw a picture of the business and design the data base according to this picture. If the total box or picture represents the business environment, then it becomes relatively easy to fill in the blanks or topic areas. Think of each line of business as a separate topic area. Figure 7-1 is an example.

With a sample design, menus can be built to access each topic area in addition to having access to the entire data base. Clearly, key word search techniques are applied to the software to retrieve the information. One word of caution: The data base should be designed by the business executive with assistance from the information systems staff or outside consultants. The design should be flexible because the business environment will continue to change, as may the structure of the organization. Companies continually acquire and divest businesses. Intelligence systems must take these factors into consideration. Information from the field and international information should be included in the data base design. These topics are discussed in detail in Chapters 8 and 9, respectively.

Integration Issues

In addition to data base design, there are integration factors involved in bringing a shared information network to fruition. These issues relate to the actual physical building of the system from both technical and nontechnical aspects and system maintenance.

Software

It should be emphasized that software and hardware decisions should be made after the design and development of the intelligence system. These systems are end user based,

Figure 7-1.   Sample data base design for a major money center bank.

```
┌─────────────────────────────────────────────────────────┐
│  External Information                                    │
│  Newspapers, journals, other publications               │
├─────────────────────────────────────────────────────────┤
│  Financial Services Industry                            │
│                                                         │
│  Domestic                                               │
│   Banking industry                                      │
│    Money center banks                                   │
│    Regional activity                                    │
│   Nonbanks                                              │
│   Securities industry                                   │
│   Insurance industry                                    │
│   International                                         │
├─────────────────────────────────────────────────────────┤
│  Impact of Technology on the Financial Services Industry│
│  Hardware                                               │
│  Software                                               │
│  Telecommunications                                     │
├─────────────────────────────────────────────────────────┤
│  Internal Information                                   │
│  Library catalog documents                              │
│  Market research reports                                │
│  Strategic planning documents                           │
│  Internal meetings, speeches                            │
│  Product development information                        │
├─────────────────────────────────────────────────────────┤
│  Field Intelligence (for example, information from      │
│                      sales representatives)             │
└─────────────────────────────────────────────────────────┘
```

and the content of the information should not be dependent on system constraints. For example, intelligence systems typically involve textual information. Because most of the information is "soft" information, or information obtained from periodicals, newspapers, and other media, the majority of these corporate systems require text retrieval software designed for either the mainframe or personal computer, or both.

A major food company had designed and developed an intelligence system around a specific software package that was already purchased by the company. The system development required hundreds of hours of manpower in terms of indexing the material for input to the system. After two years, few users were accessing the system because of the difficulty of access and complexity of the software. A decision was made to scrap the data base and temporarily revert to a hard copy intelligence newsletter service. The company is now delaying any decision to transfer the new files to any type of system until end-user requirements are fully evaluated.

As these systems become more sophisticated, many companies are attempting to integrate textual and numeric information. To meet this need, relational data base software vendors are expanding their text retrieval capabilities. Additionally, software vendors are developing full-scale software packages called executive information systems (EISs).

An EIS simplifies access to large quantities of information by translating hard copy to electronic data. Because such systems are distributed by high-powered computers, these types of data bases are intended to accelerate communication. (This is what has made electronic mail an important function of any shared information network.) EISs are intended to change the way people think because the information that comprises an EIS system is diverse and not routinely available in paper reports. For a large organization with more than 1,000 employees at one site, such systems may include sales and marketing information (such as that provided by syndicated research firms like A. C. Nielsen), human resource information, internal financial data, and so on. Some EISs allow users to do "what-if" analyses and on-screen forecasting, as well as build graphs and charts from textual information on the screen. Thus, an EIS brings a variety of data to the desk tops of key executives. Moreover, many such systems are ideal for integrating key internal and external information sources. These packages are intended to function as one-stop-shopping mechanisms for retrieval of information from multiple data bases. Whatever the industry buzzwords, software vendors are becoming increasingly responsive to the need for customized software that integrates information sources.

A problem with these sophisticated systems is that they are marketed as a solution to all business problems. In addition, many organizations require that their EIS application be customized to their specific needs. As a result, it can be difficult for the software vendor and the organization to decipher what type of information should go into the system.

Nonetheless, EISs and other distributed information systems have made tremendous inroads in convincing senior management of the need for a corporatewide information base. It has been estimated that total sales of personal computer–based EISs will reach upward of $16 million by the mid-1990s. Currently, such systems tend to distribute data that are highly quantitative in scope. Companies are making significant investments in terms of capital and human resources in these systems, however, and are continually attempting to identify additional data sources for them.

The technologies involved in developing a shared information network will change throughout the life of the system. Therefore, software and hardware decisions should be made in stages. Because the strategic objectives of the firm may change over time, it is wise to avoid costly software development charges at the beginning of the system. These systems evolve over several years, so modifications and further enhancements can be added at a later date.

For example, when developing a shared information network, the market research department of a major money center bank made the software and hardware decisions in three phases. The first phase entailed accessing external and internal information on a stand-alone personal computer. By "stand-alone," I mean that the computer was not linked or connected to other computers or to a host computer. The market research department accessed the information through a simple text retrieval software package. The software cost only about $1,200 and was installed on a computer that was already part of the department.

After about six months of access, Phase II was begun, which entailed transferring the information to a mainframe system that was part of an existing time-sharing network within the bank. It was estimated that the total cost of the system, including manpower, system maintenance, and modifications, was $30,000 a year. After about one year of having this information available on a mainframe, it was decided to transfer the shared information network to a newly designed relational data base management/executive information system that was set up for the entire organization. On an annual basis, Phase III costs $60,000 to $80,000. For the market research department and the entire bank, this phased approach was key as it fostered information sharing and communication between various departments.

Computers

Of course, a corporate or departmental computer is required for large-scale systems that will be accessed by multiple departments and multiple users. Information system executives are now building capacity requirements into their plans for these systems. For departmental intelligence systems, these files can be accessed from the corporate computer or shared information network. Initial prototyping should be executed on a personal computer and then transferred to the corporate computer or mainframe.

As companies seek to develop a system architecture that can access multiple data bases (including both textual and numeric), the hardware and software issues become more significant. Overall, the design of intelligence systems should not be subordinated to the computer or software requirements.

Data Base Integrity Issues

By this time, you ought to be asking the following questions:

Who will maintain the data base?
How do we maintain integrity of the data base?
What internal resources are required to execute the project?

It is clear that corporate intelligence data bases or networks must be maintained and administered, for best results, by a single department. This department should work closely with end users and screen information for input into the system. Additionally, this group should be responsible for end-user training and feedback.

Despite the size of some of these systems, even the largest can be managed by a staff of no more than two full-time administrative professionals. In terms of data base maintenance, competitive intelligence information should be kept for a period of at least two years. After a period of five years of updates, the information should be archived by use of another storage mechanism, such as compact disc-read only memory (CD-ROM) technology.

Cost of the System

The cost of a shared information network may sound like quite an investment. Yet, in an intensely competitive business environment, it is necessary to weigh the expense of an ongoing tracking system that effectively integrates internal and external information sources against the cost of lost market share or a missed new product opportunity.

The total cost of a system can be broken down as follows:

- System development costs
- System maintenance
- Future enhancements

System development costs include the cost of selecting the information content, designing the system, and prototyping. Clearly, the costs for development on a personal computer are significantly lower than for mainframe system development. Internal staff time should also be factored into the cost. For personal computer systems, development costs can range from $10,000 to $50,000. For complex corporate computer systems, development costs can range from $50,000 to $100,000 (excluding software and hardware acquisition cost).

For maintenance of these systems, it is necessary to factor in the salaries of the administrative staff dedicated to the system. Additionally, the cost of the external information should be included in this cost. For personal computer systems the cost usually runs from $25,000 to $50,000 and for corporate computer systems from $100,000 to $200,000 in annual operating expenses.

Companies are most likely to implement enhancements to the system after a period of success. These enhancements may range from transferring the system to a mainframe to expanding the content of the data base to include international information or field intelligence. Enhancements are typically made to mainframe systems in increments of $25,000 to $35,000.

Chapter 12 contains a detailed discussion of tying the system to the bottom line. Small firms attempting to get started with this process might consider implementing the process in hard copy, which could include a newsletter or reporting system. Here, the decision to make or buy depends on the level of expertise in the company. Generally, small to medium firms do not employ large staffs of analysts, nor do they have a full-service library with hundreds of newspapers and subscriptions. Thus, it is beneficial to these firms to "buy" industry and market intelligence in the form of newsletters and tracking services that offer current research reports. These may range from $500 annually to $2,000 to $5,000 for research reports.

Evolution of the Data Base

Intelligence systems should be built somewhat as a house is built. First, the plans should be drawn up and the foundation laid. Second, the basic elements of the system should be put into production. Specifically, this entails capturing and disseminating information that has the highest impact on the business. Third, additional sections or topic areas should be added to the data base, depending on end-user feedback and the changing business conditions of the organization.

Ford Motor Company— Corporate Technical Information System

Ford Motor Company recognized that automotive technology is in an era in which rapid advances are being made each year. With the globalization of the industry, the amount of publicly available literature about technological developments is expanding at an increasing rate. As such, the engineers and analysts within the industry are faced with the dilemma of being aware of all these sources of information while being able to access only the information relevant to their tasks. Although commercial data bases have proliferated over the past decade, their high cost, difficult access and usage regimens, and lack of automotive specificity led Ford Motor Company to develop its own data base system.

Ford recognized the need to more efficiently collect, evaluate, and disseminate product and technical information in 1983. A small staff was organized to investigate this need. Supported by representatives of potential users throughout the company, a plan to create an in-house computerized system was developed in 1984. The principal objective was to allow the user to address two types of information need. General questions such as, What developments in ceramic engine applications are coming out of Japan? would be covered by a technical information data base. Specific questions like, What is the range of the wheelbases of all cars in the subcompact class? would be addressed by a facts and figures data base.

Clearly, what was needed was a custom library on every desk that could be tailored to every task. The library had to have a large capacity to grow and had to be accessible from everywhere. It had to be flexible enough to operate with little more than its own on-screen instructions, yet allow instantaneous data retrieval with high precision. Moreover, it had to be up to date and the content had to be automotive-specific.

System Development. The development of the Ford system, called the Corporate Technical Information System (CTIS), began in mid-1984. Four user-driven goals were established for guiding the overall direction of the system:

- Make the system extremely user friendly.
- Make the system up to date.
- Draw the content from sources worldwide.
- Provide fast, easy access to the data from company locations worldwide.

To meet the development goals, Honeywell Multics System at the Ford Engineering Computer Center was chosen because of its established multiuser worldwide network. A new text software program, TEXTO, was selected for the text data bases. MRDS, or Multics Relational Data Store, was selected as the appropriate software for the numbers-intensive Facts and Figures Database.

In developing the Technical Information Database, the first task was to analyze the data sources. Worldwide product and technical information was evaluated and some twenty-five periodicals and journals were selected as primary sources. A decision to include only abstracts of the relevant articles was made to conserve computer storage space.

Access to the data base was made user friendly through the natural query language of TEXTO and identifier fields that enabled each and every word in the data file to become searchable. Ford cited the benefit of using an index file for searching because of the speed of response. User interfaces, or menus, were then created. These programs prompt the user with a series of options, structure the user's inputs into data base queries, execute the queries, and report the results.

Once the user has completed a search, several options become available. Because most users use microcomputers with modems to access the data base, viewing the data on a terminal is a frequent selection. The communications software at the local level generally allows the user to download what is seen on the screen to a local file for hard copy printing at the user's location. Another option is to have the mainframe print a copy of the search results for delivery to the user.

In addition to abstracting done locally, material is received from Ford Technical Liaison personnel in Europe and Japan. These two sources have proven very valuable in supplying information that is virtually unobtainable from conventional domestic and overseas sources. A test launch of the data base was conducted in January 1985 with full release to all company personnel in April 1985.

Current Progress. Since the launch, the number of users, as well as the breadth and depth of the Technical Information Database, has grown dramatically. The data base has more than 1,400 users, and the number of literature sources has been expanded to more than 150. In addition, more than 22,000 records are now in the data base and new data are now being added at the rate of 12,000 records per year.

The success and acceptance of the Technical Information Database has led to user demand for more and varied file types. From the initial concept of two information data bases, the system has grown to eighteen files.

During 1987, a survey of CTIS users was conducted. The survey found that

- 79 percent of the users thought CTIS aided them in doing their job;

- 38 percent indicated CTIS saved them time;
- 14 percent said its use resulted in cost savings; and most important,
- 24 percent indicated CTIS has already led to improved quality.

The survey also identified two problems:

1. The need for improved customer services
2. A demand for significantly expanded system content

In response to these findings, customer services were upgraded with an improved customer interface, specifically, the addition of "help" selection alternatives in each menu. Additionally, more sophisticated search software was applied to the system to enhance user friendliness. Additional files have been added, including data files from external vendors. This adds strategic content to the data base and complements the internal information.

Benefits of the System. CTIS provides its users with single-point access to the integration of internal and external information sources. The data have both a strategic and tactical focus and are easy to access and up to date. CTIS is continually evolving as the administrators are continually receiving and prioritizing user requests for new files and file content. As such, CTIS is a state-of-the-art corporate intelligence data base that has been in successful operation since 1985. More important, it is customized to the needs of the firm. CTIS is available to every Ford business and market analyst, every Ford engineer and technician, and thousands of company people worldwide. Potentially, there are thousands of others who might profit from its use.[1]

---

[1]Copyright 1987 Society of Automotive Engineers, Inc., SAE Technical Paper Series 871927, "The Corporate Technical Information System: The Ford Inhouse Information Utility Passenger Car Meeting and Exposition," Dearborn, Michigan, October 19–22, 1987. Reprinted with permission.

Summary

Nearly all executives are faced with the challenge of obtaining timely information about their business environment. Most executives, however, do not have a single-point access system for obtaining this information on a daily basis. In reality, a majority of executives and key department personnel have to read newspapers and journals, attend meetings, be part of the corporate routing list, or rely on information from field settings.

Ford's information network was initially driven by the tracking of technology. Afterward, the company's cost-efficient methodology of adding users (by division) and sources (by topic area) helped ensure the continued survival and utility of the system. CTIS is a corporate intelligence system designed to meet the business objectives of the firm. Even though it is a large-scale system, CTIS meets the needs of diverse end users (manufacturing, R&D, product development, marketing, and planning staff).

Clearly, most organizations are not as large as and do not have the resources of Ford. Smaller organizations may only require the input of a few departments that contribute to the system. Also, small companies may not require the development of a sophisticated computer system to distribute the information; a hard copy reporting system or newsletter may suffice nicely. This underscores the point that a shared information network does not have to be as highly structured and complex as a multiuser mainframe system.

The markets and business environment for companies in some industries are not technology-intensive and are more consumer-driven (for example, health and beauty aids). For building an intelligence network, these organizations focus more on the actual end-use markets and the external business environment. For instance, in the health and beauty aids industry, intelligence gathering and information from field settings are a major facet of the system. The notion of field intelligence is discussed in detail in Chapter 8.

8

Field Intelligence Systems

"Knowledge is the only instrument of production that is not subject to diminishing returns."

John Maurice Clark, Columbia University

Although a tremendous amount of business and competitive information exists in soft, externally published sources, the most timely information exists in the field, that is, in work environments like distribution, selling, manufacturing, research and development, and technical settings. In many field environments, information develops on a first-hand basis even before the media or another party becomes involved.

Some of this information from the field may be rumors, but it is still worth reporting, because a sizable amount of published competitive information is not made available on a timely basis. Sometimes, such information is made available to key executives as much as sixty to ninety days after it is published. For this reason, tracking and monitoring field information and integrating it into a shared information network acts as an additional source of vital information and can give organizations a competitive edge.

The Value of Field Intelligence

Field intelligence has a significant impact on the concept of information sharing. Oftentimes, valuable tactical and strategic information is "lost" because notes are kept in the minds or the briefcases of field personnel or plant personnel. Field intelligence that is integrated into a shared information network can be an effective way to monitor the pricing, distribution, sales and marketing, and product activities of competitors, industries, and markets.

Thus, the challenge for today's business executives remains how to capture field intelligence and how to integrate it into a shared information network.

Oftentimes, field intelligence contains information that is not found in published form. Here are some common types of field intelligence:

- New product development activity
- New plant investment activity
- Promotional activity

- Management changes
- Sales force activity
- Pricing information
- Changes in strategy

Field information can be obtained about any of these items. Consider this hypothetical example:

Staying Ahead of the Competition

John Atkins, a representative of the research and development unit of Company X, a major soap manufacturer, was talking to one of the company's chemical suppliers, William Hansen, over the telephone. Over the years, Atkins had obtained a good rapport with Hansen and even communicated with him on a first-name basis.

In discussing newly available chemicals for soaps, Hansen touted the chemical company's new surfactant, which can result in an ideal facial soap for sensitive skin that allows manufacturers to garner high margins. After the two discussed the properties and benefits of the new surfactant, Atkins asked Hansen, "What has the response been from your other customers?"

Hansen said that he had heard, from a well-informed company source, that Company Y, another soap manufacturer and Company X's major competitor, purchased a two-year supply of the surfactant. Hansen added that he heard that Company Y would use the chemical to introduce a new brand of facial soap for sensitive skin that comes in a pump dispenser.

After taking notes on this, Atkins quickly called corporate headquarters to tell key personnel of the field intelligence that he had found. As it turned out, Company Y did introduce the facial soap for sensitive skin about two months after Atkins's phone conversation with Hansen. In that time span, however, Company X was able to respond to the field intelligence by purchasing the new surfactant from the chemical company and incorporating it in an existing brand of bar soap. Thus, Company X not only used this field intelligence to develop a similar product, but did so by using an existing brand name, thereby saving money in marketing and advertising expenditures.

Clearly, information from the field is gathered by word of mouth. Competitive intelligence does not mean corporate espionage, although there may be some situations that will require you to seek legal counsel with regard to reporting and disseminating this type of information. A methodology for capturing, organizing, and disseminating this type of information follows.

How to Implement
Field Intelligence Programs

Field intelligence systems require top–down support or commitment from senior management. Because the success of these systems depends on a significant effort from those employees in field settings, the field personnel must view the development of this system as critical to the company's operations. The methodology that I have developed entails a five-step process:

Step 1.   Incentive to Contribute to the System
Step 2.   Content, Format, and Focus of the Information

Step 3.   Dissemination of the Information
Step 4.   Integration of Internal or Field Sales Infor-
            mation With Externally Published Infor-
            mation
Step 5.   The Feedback Process

Step 1: Incentive to Contribute to the System

Because of their significant time constraints and traditional
aversion to paperwork, the employees in field settings have
probably the most difficult functions from which to secure
commitment for an intelligence-gathering effort. For this
reason, incentives must be built into the field intelligence
gathering process. Examples of these incentives include the
following:

- Incorporate the intelligence-gathering function as a
  part of the field employee's job.
- Provide recognition for specific field personnel who
  take the time to contribute to the field intelligence
  gathering effort.
- Compensate field personnel for this function.

Field intelligence personnel can gain recognition
within an organization through various means. For instance,
an organization with a relatively large number of field
employees (one hundred or more) can develop an employee
award that recognizes the information-gathering efforts of
an employee on a weekly or monthly basis. For organizations with a small number of field personnel, such an award
can be given on a less frequent basis (semiannually or
annually). These incentive awards can be cash money (bo-
nuses, merit increases) or other inducements (extra vacation
time, free trips, tickets to a ball game).

Clearly, each company has its own marketing and sales
culture and structure. Many firms have creatively and effectively used incentives to develop field intelligence systems.

Step 2: Content, Format, and Focus of the Information

Field intelligence systems require focusing on the potential impact of information on the business. Clearly, these systems are not intended to dilute the sales, manufacturing, or distribution efforts of the company. However, it is imperative that field personnel know what the key field intelligence needs of an organization are. Typically, these needs are those listed at the start of this chapter under "The Value of Field Intelligence." At this point, you may be asking the question, How do I focus on the key field intelligence needs of my organization?

Because field personnel are closely associated with the external sales and marketing environment, more so than corporate staff, they must adhere to a "macro" approach when focusing on information needs. This broader environment includes the competitors (both existing and potential) of an organization, the products and services (both existing and potential) of the organization and its competitors, and the interrelationships between field personnel and their customers (wholesalers, retailers, and consumers). For instance, a pharmaceutical salesperson should become "field smart" with regard to the following questions:

Competition

Who are our existing competitors?
Who are our potential competitors?

Products/Services

What products/services are we marketing that the competition is not?
What products/services is the competition marketing that we are?
What products/services is the competition marketing that we are not?
What are the policies of the competition regarding pricing, selling, distribution, customer service, customer ordering, dealing with back orders, and so on?

Customers

How do my customers perceive me and the organization that I represent?

What is the status of the relationships between me and my customers (hospitals, private practices, health care institutions, and so on)?

How, if at all, can I gather intelligence from my customers?

Is my customer base growing, stagnating, or declining?

External Environment

What external factors can affect my intelligence-gathering efforts and sales (for example, economic growth, health of consumers, and budgets of health care institutions)?

It is more effective to gather intelligence on a few items that have a significant impact on the business than to ask managers and employees who work in field settings to gather anything they can find. Here is an example of key information elements, which can be incorporated in a simple one-page format:

- Date
- Competitor news
  —New product development/line extension
  —Pricing
  —Promotion/merchandising techniques
  —Dealer offerings
- Source of information
- Action to be taken

Because most field intelligence is received verbally, it should be entered on the information sheet while it is being gathered or soon thereafter. Moreover, the information should be entered into the shared information network. The format should be kept consistent between field personnel and the network to increase efficiency and make it easier for the internal champion and the task force to input field intelligence effectively and on a timely basis.

Format of the Information

The format of the information is key to field intelligence systems. Depending on the primary focus of the business, the information can be organized by line of business, sales region, or competitor. Picture this potential system as a hard copy report with tabs. Once you decide how the information should be organized, the design and groundwork of the intelligence system becomes relatively easy.

By Line of Business. Line of business is probably the most popular way of organizing field intelligence because information on both competitors and markets can be easily captured by segmenting the report by line of business. Nowadays, such a format (see Figure 8-1) is widely used because most organizations are in several lines of business and management can easily locate competitor news by selecting a product line.

By Sales Region. Alternatively, sales and marketing personnel may want to organize competitive information by sales region (Figure 8-2). With this focus, they may want to track a competitor's strategies on a regional basis. Such a format is useful for corporations adopting regional marketing programs. In a growing number of corporations, sales departments are segmented by geographic area or region and are given more autonomy, responsibility, and accountability. This allows departments to focus on the marketing aspects of a particular geographic area or region.

By Competitor. In some industries, corporations compete on a national and a global basis, which makes it worthwhile to focus on intelligence gathering by competitor (Figure 8-3). For instance, many of the large food companies compete in a variety of food industries and market products

Figure 8-1. Field intelligence by line of business.

Line of Business: _____

Competitor: _____

News: _____

_____

_____

_____

Source: _____

Sales Region: _____

Action to Be Taken: _____

_____

_____

Figure 8-2. Field intelligence by sales region.

Sales Region: _____

Line of Business: _____

Competitor: _____

News: _____

_____

_____

_____

Source: _____

Action to Be Taken: _____

_____

_____

Figure 8-3. Field intelligence by competitor.

```
┌─────────────────────────────────────────────────────┐
│                                                       │
│  Competitor: _____      │
│  Line of Business: _____     │
│  News: _____      │
│                                                       │
│        _____      │
│        _____      │
│        _____      │
│                                                       │
│  Source: _____      │
│  Sales Region: _____      │
│  Action to Be Taken: _____      │
│                                                       │
│        _____      │
│        _____      │
│                                                       │
└─────────────────────────────────────────────────────┘
```

on a global basis. As such, it can be very difficult to gather field intelligence by line of business or sales region. In such industries, gathering field intelligence by competitor is more effective than other formats. In fact, such a format has become more and more popular as corporations have embraced the concepts of systematically tracking their competitors, the so-called notion of competitive intelligence.

Many "exception reporting" systems, which focus on the competition as a separate project, are designed in this manner.

Timeliness of the Information

Timeliness of field intelligence is essential and is what makes field intelligence valuable. Field intelligence information should be captured and integrated into a shared information network daily or weekly to capitalize on the lead time over published information. There are three major methods for capturing field intelligence:

- One-page flash report
- Electronic transmission from the field directly to a data base
- By telephone to a central coordinator or internal champion

One-Page Flash Report. The one-page flash report is a simple, low-cost, and efficient method for field personnel to gather intelligence. Such a report can be generated on a daily or weekly basis. Because it forces the field intelligence gatherer to think about what he or she writes, the quality of the information is usually high and well thought out. On the other hand, field personnel who are pressed for time and have an aversion to paperwork are likely not to contribute to this process, unless they can be compelled to do so. This is where the use of incentives can be an effective part of a field intelligence system.

Electronic Transmission From the Field Directly to a Data Base. With the advent of portable lap-top computers and hand-held terminals, field personnel can efficiently load timely information into the system. The advantage of this method is that the information can be transmitted from the field to the network on a very timely basis, usually right after the intelligence is gathered or daily. A central coordinator is usually needed, however, to screen the input for quality control of the data.

Telephone Information to a Central Coordinator. Several marketing and sales departments have set up a procedure whereby field personnel phone significant competitive events to a central coordinator on a daily or weekly basis. The central coordinator then integrates the information into a weekly or monthly report or newsletter. Here again, even though this system ensures the timeliness of the information, specific details on interpretations of the data may not be clearly communicated in a telephone conversation.

Step 3: Dissemination of the Information

Field intelligence should be captured on a daily basis, input upon receipt, and disseminated weekly or twice a month. The following are some methods for dissemination of the information:

- Weekly/monthly newsletter
- Monthly marketing report
- Electronic data base
  —Personal computer
  —Dial-up system (domestic and international)

Weekly/Monthly Newsletter. Within corporations, many sales and marketing departments publish a weekly or monthly newsletter that recaps competitive activity, new product announcements, promotional activity, and so forth. These reports are very useful—if, and only if, they are published on a timely basis. The content of the information must be actionable, thus allowing management to make proactive business decisions on the basis of the newsletter. Weekly or monthly intelligence newsletters can take various forms. Appendix K provides an example of a monthly newsletter for a manufacturer and distributor of frozen vegetables.

Monthly Marketing Report. Most organizations require that their sales or marketing department publish a monthly report that recaps account performance, market share data, competitive activity, and so on. Field intelligence is often integrated into these reports. Because these reports require extensive coordination between internal marketing and product line staffs, the reporting process is often cumbersome and the reports are often issued late. Moreover, these reports are typically issued "up" the organization to senior management, rather than being fed back to the field.

Electronic Data Base. During the past few years, several companies have capitalized on the new lap-top and hand-held terminal technology and initiated a process to streamline data capturing and reporting. Data can be captured in a variety of electronic and nonelectronic formats and fed into a local region or corporate staff for reformatting for various reporting systems. The following company's story describes this type of system.

Domestic Field Intelligence for Insurance Executives

Personnel at a major insurance company were becoming increasingly aware of their competitive environment as the lines were fading between traditional financial service products for consumers. Their major problem was developing a system or a process that would capture field information on a timely basis. The structure of their field sales force was complex. Additionally, the competitive information was in two formats: text information for description of new competitive products, and numeric data for competitive rates.

Following a strategic information audit, the company determined that a process was needed to capture information on a systematic basis and disseminate it in a report format on a timely basis. Field representatives were interviewed to determine the content, format, frequency of update, and method of transmission of field intelligence. In this case, input had to be captured daily because new product announcements were made and rates changed on a daily basis. Because time is the most valuable asset of field representatives, a process had to be established that would input data to the system on a daily basis. More important, a reward system had to be established that would encourage information reporting from the field.

To meet the reporting requirements, the corporate marketing department, with the assistance of a consulting firm, established a one-page intelligence sheet that contained information on the source, the regional office, competitive new product descriptions, and competitive rates. Second, the local office allocated the time of a local administrative person to enter the information onto a local terminal on a daily basis. Third, incentives were built into the commission structure for active participation in the field intelligence reporting program.

Although the field administrator had other job duties, it was determined that he or she would spend approximately one or two hours a day inputting this type of information. When the administrator input the text and numeric data from one sheet, the system was designed to channel the text information into a new product reporting system and the numeric data into a competitive rate tracking system. The information was then transmitted to the mainframe at the corporate headquarters, which integrated the field news on a daily basis into the competitive intelligence data base. Thus, as current field intelligence became available, the system was updated and could be accessed by field reps the following day. With this tool, the field reps could now receive information on competitive rates and new product offerings to enable them to better position their products or services (see Figure 8-4). The product rates changed more frequently than the product offerings, so the company decided to segment the data bases to provide for this "real time" information.

Within a period of six to nine months following the prototype of the system, these tangible benefits were cited:

- Knowledge of current new product development activity
- Current competitive rate information on which to base pricing decisions
- Data upon which to analyze competitors' marketing strategy

Figure 8-4.   Incorporating field rep intelligence into the electronic data base.

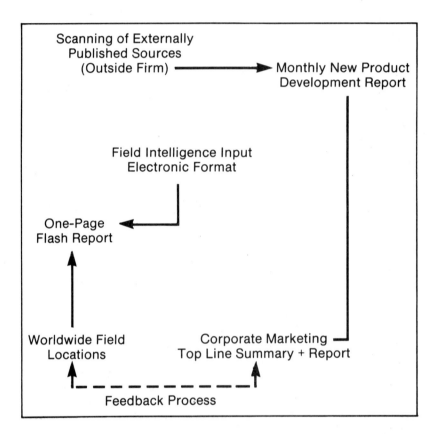

Clearly, the system proved to be a valuable tool in terms of new product development and pricing. Moreover, it has been reported that the system has more than paid for itself by the savings in delayed pricing actions. Additionally, the financial incentive in the commission structure for the field reps has encouraged a high rate of participation in the system.

Management has realized, however, that the next step is to integrate information from published sources into the data base. Although published sources may not be as timely, they include valuable advertisements of promotional campaigns for product offerings. To meet this objective, the company has contracted with an outside firm to scan relevant outside sources for input into the corporate data base. The next case discusses the integration of field intelligence with published information.

Step 4: *Integration of Internal or Field Sales Information With Externally Published Information*

Many companies have recognized that the combination of field intelligence and external information sources results in a powerful information network. Most information reported from the field is at least sixty to ninety days ahead of published competitive intelligence. Integrating this field intelligence with published information provides:

- Validation of the credibility of the field source
- Assessment of the value or the timeliness of information from published sources
- Actionable information for price moves, new product development activity, and so forth, with a higher degree of confidence from the combination of both those sources

Global Field Intelligence
for Consumer Packaged Goods Executives

A major consumer packaged goods company recognized the need to establish a process for capturing competitive information from its field on a worldwide basis, and to integrate the information with synthesized, digested information from a wide range of external sources. Because this system involved more than fifty countries worldwide, it did not make sense to impose a process of entering the international field information into a standard personal computer or software package. To capture this information, corporate marketing issued a one-page flash report to the field offices that contained competitor new product development and announcement activity. Because the firm was diversified over many lines of business, the reports could easily be put into a data base that organized the information by that variable.

In this case, global intelligence is critical not only to the corporate marketing department, but to the field locations as well. Therefore, the reward system for contributing information was designed to obtain global intelligence from the other (approximately fifty) countries. Only personnel in those countries that contributed to the system were eligible to receive the monthly new product intelligence report. Also, most of the field locations did not possess large libraries with several people scanning the literature for published new product announcements. So a reward system was established whereby for the input of one or two flash reports a month, a field location could obtain a timely, comprehensive worldwide new product development scan of all competitive activity, organized by line of business.

The company contracted with an outside electronic information provider to forward the one-page flash reports into the firm for electronic input to the system. Additionally, the outside firm simultaneously scanned, synthesized, and digested select new product development activity for the various lines of business on a daily basis for input to the system. In short, the electronic information provider integrated the company's internal field sales information with external information to produce a customized and focused report.

Timeliness was critical to the value of this report. As such, it was issued to the consumer packaged goods firm during the first week of each month. The internal coordinator then drafted a top line summary and sent the summary and the report back to the field locations that contributed to the report (Figure 8-5). If field locations were negligent in contributing to the global new product report over a period of time, they were omitted from receiving it. Moreover, the

Figure 8-5. Integrated field sales and external information system.

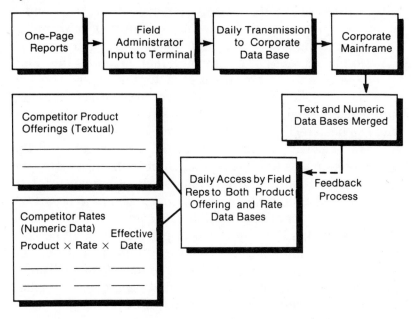

top line summary each month indicated the participating field locations and was distributed to senior management. Although this may be perceived as a negative incentive, it works.

This information system resulted in a high degree of participation from the field locations. The content, format, and timeliness of the report were strong incentives for the field offices to continue their participation in the process. More important, it was noted that tactical decisions, such as pricing and promotion strategy, were made as a result of the customized global new product report.

Step 5: The Feedback Process

The feedback process is essential to the success of information systems. You can clearly see from the last two cases how feedback on a timely basis is critical to field personnel.

The feedback process is usually handled by a central coordinator. To ensure feedback the central coordinator, after gathering intelligence from the field, should send a letter to those personnel who have submitted field intelligence thanking them for doing so. A copy of the report, newsletter, or one-page summary that includes this field intelligence should be enclosed with the letter. The key here is to make the intelligence gatherer aware that this summary is being distributed to all divisions and that he or she has been recognized as the source of the intelligence.

Another way to ensure feedback is through use of the telephone. Just as field personnel gather intelligence for the central coordinator, the central coordinator may want to call field personnel to give feedback about a report or newsletter that contains intelligence from the field.

Finally, it is important that upper management be kept abreast of how the field intelligence system is working. The central coordinator and the task force may want to arrange for meetings with upper management on a quarterly basis to give and receive feedback. Oftentimes, field personnel may even be an integral part of such a meeting.

Summary

Intelligence systems should continue to evolve. As the business and competitive environment changes, so should the system. For instance, as corporations expand and move into new lines of business or increase critical mass through acquisition, field intelligence systems can become global in scope. For organizations that are downsizing, such systems can evolve into an effective intelligence-gathering effort that is tightly focused.

9

Monitoring International Information

"An individual without information cannot take responsibility; an individual who is given information cannot help but take responsibility."

Jan Carlzon, Scandinavian Airlines

It is rare that a company in the United States today is not faced with foreign competition. In some industries and markets, such as the automotive and electronics industries, U.S. corporations have lost domestic market share. As a result, a growing number of corporations are viewing their competitive environment on a global basis. In addition, they are systematically monitoring competitors based in Europe, Asia, and other areas of the globe, competitors that have made inroads in U.S. markets as well as those that may. Tracking international competition and markets has become an integral part of shared information networks for many U.S. corporations.

In monitoring competition and markets abroad, there is no better example than Japan. Although "half of the foreign investment in Japan comes from the United States, Japanese direct investment represents about 12 percent of all foreign direct investment in the United States. Almost 250,000 Americans are working for Japanese companies in the

United States, while some 100,000 Japanese work for American firms in Japan."[1] Clearly, the United States is viewed as the world's largest consumer market, providing more liquidity and investment opportunities than any other country.

Changes are currently taking place that will have broad-based implications for organizations that do business overseas and monitor the activities of their competitors. In Europe, measures are already being taken to remove inter-European restrictions on the movement of money, goods, and people between the member countries of the European Economic Community. By 1992, Europe will become a unified market. Such prospects have already affected many industries, and cross-border mergers and corporate reorganizations in anticipation of 1992 are at record levels. In addition, such a common market will increase the depth and breadth of information that is available from published European sources and the amount of field intelligence that is sourced and distributed.

Rather than tracking a handful of domestic competitors competing for market share in many segmented and mature markets, a growing number of domestic organizations are asking the question, What are foreign competitors doing to penetrate our U.S. markets? Most experienced planning professionals and analysts will agree that this is a difficult question to answer. In order to conduct competitive tracking on a global basis, an organization must establish a methodology for gathering foreign competitive information and placing this information into a shared information network.

A methodology for gathering international competitive information and incorporating this information into the planning process is presented in this chapter. Examples that demonstrate the effectiveness of these techniques are presented.

---

[1]Excerpted from a *TIME* Magazine Special Advertising Section "Investing in the Global Economy." © 1989 The Time Inc. Magazine Company.

The Need for a Formal Process

Before an organization decides to develop a global competitive intelligence gathering program, the following questions should be answered:

1. *Is your company already manufacturing and marketing its products and services internationally?* Many U.S. corporations are called multinationals and do business in all corners of the globe, and some only do business in select international markets. Clearly, a growing number of corporations based in the United States manufacture, distribute, and market their products and services overseas and have become multinationals. Those that do so already have an upper hand in tracking their competitors, industries, and markets on a global scale.

2. *Is your company purchasing or manufacturing any of its components or raw materials in other countries?* In some industries, many American corporations are buying or manufacturing overseas raw materials and components that go into making finished products, then exporting these materials or finished products to the United States. They do this because it is less costly to manufacture raw materials or finished products overseas and then ship them to the United States than to manufacture them here. This tactic has become especially prevalent in the automotive industry, in which companies are manufacturing components and subassemblies in newly industrialized countries (for example, South Korea) and in countries where the cost of labor is much lower than in the United States.

3. *Is your company vulnerable to large profit swings as a result of currency devaluations?* Because there is no one currency used on a global basis, organizations that do business overseas can be affected by currency fluctuations in a particular country. For instance, over the past decade or so, the value of the Japanese yen has appreciated substantially vis-à-vis the U.S. dollar and other currencies. In various industries, this appreciation has made it much more difficult to do business in Japan. This situation is one of the

reasons Japanese auto manufacturers are now manufacturing more of their automobiles in the United States, Europe, and other countries, while manufacturing fewer in Japan.

4. *Does your company's track record abroad compare well to its success in domestic markets?* It is widely accepted that the best measurement of future performance is past performance. Yet, domestic success may or may not determine success abroad. Various case studies have documented this fact. Thus, organizations may or may not be successful if they decide to export their domestic products and services. Many organizations have experienced failure in attempting to do this. However, as companies learn from past mistakes, expand their interests abroad through internal expansion or acquisition, and learn more about the cultural and psychological differences between the United States and other countries, they will develop good track records. Many organizations have already done so.

5. *Has your company achieved global brand identification or loyalty?* Many U.S. multinationals have been able to increase global awareness of and loyalty to a particular brand name or product. For instance, on almost every continent, when consumers are asked to list computer manufacturers, it is safe to say that most respondents would place IBM at the top of that list. If the same consumers were asked, What brand do you identify most with disposable diapers? most respondents would probably say Pampers. It can take many years to achieve such status. Initially, it may be best to limit one's focus to a particular geographic area or region.

6. *Have international competitors begun to chip away at your domestic market share?* As a growing number of corporations from Europe, Japan, and elsewhere are expanding their interests in the United States, many American organizations are experiencing a decline in market share. Unilever, a Dutch and British company, is one of the largest consumer products companies in the world. During the late 1980s, the company exponentially increased its interests in

the household, personal care, and fragrance markets of the United States through internal expansion and acquisition.

All these questions are pivotal considering the changes that are occurring in Europe. For instance, many companies that do business overseas have established or expanded their manufacturing and distribution capabilities in Europe, and many companies that do not do business overseas are considering it. The removal of trade barriers between the European Economic Community countries will increase the amount of information available from both published sources and field settings. These prospects have made Europe an area of growth emphasis by many multinational companies.

During the 1950s and 1960s and into the 1970s, few U.S. corporations paid little more than lip service to foreign competition and the need to gather international competitive intelligence. During these decades, U.S. corporations and their respective markets were growing at a rapid rate, and the objective of most corporations was to maintain and increase domestic market share.

This trend, however, did not continue through the 1980s. Strategic planning and marketing analysts continued to revise their business plans with the same methodology and type of information that were used during the preceding three decades. As their market shares began to erode, U.S. corporations began monitoring the growth of new foreign competitors in the United States and aggressively expanding international interests. Nearly every company faced with this problem is currently looking for a methodology for tracking their foreign competitors.

Stated simply, planners of U.S. companies are faced with the following challenges involved in tracking their foreign competitors:

- The language barrier(s)
- The timeliness of information
- The lack of a quick solution to information gathering
- Patience in developing a system
- Lack of commitment from senior management

The Solution

Unfortunately, no one consulting firm or information provider has the solution neatly packaged in a product or service that you can buy. International competitive tracking programs must be developed with the expertise of internal personnel and external consultants and vendors. Moreover, these systems evolve over a period of time. As a result, they are far more complex than a shared information network or competitive intelligence program that is domestic in scope.

In addition, U.S. companies are beginning to pioneer international competitive intelligence programs. Organizations establishing these tracking systems are beginning to realize significant tangible benefits. These companies, however, have developed a methodology for systematically tracking their foreign competitors and have integrated this process with their information network and with their strategic and marketing planning functions.

Conduct an Information Audit

An international competitive effort should not be launched without first conducting an information audit that maps the company's goals and objectives against the available domestic and international information sources. Such an audit is an integral part of the strategic information audit discussed in Chapter 4. To increase efficiency and continuity, an audit that pinpoints goals and objectives and overseas information sources should be implemented concurrently with an audit that does the same for domestic information sources.

Table 9-1 shows a simple grid form that can be used to conduct an audit to monitor international information. The audit should involve input from strategic planning, market research, accounting, corporate development, and the library or information center. A series of interviews should be conducted with each of these departments to assess the internal resources available for international intelligence gathering. The questions and format of the interviews should be similar to those for the strategic information audit

Table 9-1. Information grid.

Strategic Goals		Information Sources	
Domestic	International	Domestic	International
_____	_____	_____	_____
_____	_____	_____	_____
_____	_____	_____	_____

(Chapter 4). The trigger questions used to assess the international information resources, however, are somewhat different. The following is a simple questionnaire that asks many of the same questions, but with an international scope. However, it is important that such a questionnaire be administered concurrently with one that assesses the domestic information resources of an organization.

INTERNATIONAL QUESTIONNAIRE

Date of Interview: _____

Department: _____

Interviewee: _____

Interviewer: _____

Information Sources

1. What overseas information sources do you use to obtain market intelligence or competitor intelligence?

2. How satisfied are you with these information sources as they pertain to your job function?
3. What is your budget on international information sources?
4. What publications do you subscribe to? What is the total cost of subscriptions?
5. What areas do these publications come from? What languages are they in?
6. What publications that you do not receive should be acquired?
7. What elements would make your current information sources more valuable (for example, more timely information)?

Information Distribution

8. To which overseas departments do you distribute information?
9. How frequently do you circulate information to other departments?
10. What international information sources gathered by your group would be appropriate to put into a corporatewide shared information network?

Critical Information Issues

11. What international information would you look for on a routine basis?
12. How would you like to see information indexed (by competitor, line of business, market, geographic area)?
13. What emerging technologies or competitors might threaten the market position of your group or even cause your group to be divested (for example, the European Economic Community)?

Time Factors, Expectations, and Format

14. How often would you like to see the information updated (daily, weekly, monthly, quarterly)?
15. What are your initial expectations of a business intelligence network? How will it benefit your role in the organization and your line of business?
16. In what format would you like to see the data for the network? Would you rather have summarized abstracts, abstracts with analysis, or the full text of a document?
17. How would you like to access this information (hard copy, disk)?

Other

18. What are the future needs of the network (for example, should it focus on regional markets, opportunities overseas, and more competitive policies rather than on actual products/services)?
19. What other marketing services would benefit your department or job function (for instance, qualitative research)?
20. Who else would you recommend we interview?
21. Which consulting firms have you hired over the past few years? What services have they performed and what did each firm charge?
22. Has your department used a translation service to translate foreign publications into English? Would such a service be an effective way to expedite information flow?

Of course, these are just examples. Oftentimes, the trigger questions center around the strategic goals or culture of an organization. For instance, if one of the strategic goals of the company is to introduce a new drug in a major therapeutic segment on a global basis and minimal international competitive information exists, then this is a target area for gathering international information. For this example, the information sources grid form would look something like Table 9-2.

The strategic information audit helps the internal champion and the task force to focus the international intelligence gathering effort.

Internal Information Sources

In many U.S. multinational companies, a tremendous amount of international information already exists within the firm. The problem is identifying the type of information available and the sources. The following sites generate international information:

- Domestic and international R&D labs
- International sales offices
- Domestic and foreign brokers and distributors
- Foreign affiliates
- Foreign manufacturing plants

Table 9-2. Information grid.

Strategic Goals		Information Sources	
Domestic	International	Domestic	International
Become a low-cost producer of pharmaceuticals	Introduce new drug in a major therapeutic segment on a global basis	Domestic newspapers and trade publications Field intelligence Commercial data bases	Commercial data bases Information available from regulatory agencies Published sources from countries of interest

Even though a wealth of information may exist in these locations, the information will continue to reside there in a "passive" manner unless a process is developed to extract it on a timely basis and forward it to some type of central intelligence center. This involves the effort of an internal champion or task force.

Tapping Your Foreign Offices and Affiliates

U.S. corporations with established foreign offices and affiliates have a significant advantage. From a research standpoint, they can minimize the purchase cost of competitive information from foreign research firms. In some countries, sophisticated market intelligence or research firms do not even exist. So the challenge is to establish an efficient method for transmitting timely and accurate information from international field locations. Clearly, these foreign offices will not cooperate with the effort unless the program is supported by top management.

Issues such as the type, format, and timeliness of information need to be resolved. Foreign affiliates generally do not have a library and a large staff of researchers. Most offices subscribe to a few local publications and have an administrative person who supports the local marketing or sales effort. In such cases, the affiliate or local office has the capabilities to forward competitive information and relevant news items of new product development activity, pricing announcements, plant expansions, and merger and acquisition activity. Depending on the technology available, the information is best transmitted on a daily basis via facsimile or by more sophisticated and cost-efficient methods that utilize computers (for example, electronic mail).

Overseas research and development labs, however, usually have more resources available to them. Some possess large libraries and many researchers. Whatever their size, they should be included in the global intelligence gathering effort. These organizations must clearly see the value of the effort and, more important, receive intelligence reports in return.

Timeliness and Format of the Information

The timeliness and format of the information are secondary to getting commitments from the affiliates. The timeliness issue can be best addressed by daily transmission or update of the information, if possible. What good does it do if you learn two months after an affiliate did that a foreign competitor is launching a new product in West Germany that will directly compete with your new product line?

Regarding the format of the information—keep it simple! One-page intelligence summaries are all that are needed to describe competitor new product development, promotion, or pricing activity.

Pharmaceutical Firm Capitalizes on Its Foreign Affiliates

Phase I. A major U.S. pharmaceutical firm experiencing increased competition from European firms conducted a strategic information audit and then organized a task force to gather local information from its European research and development centers and foreign affiliates.

The staff secured a commitment from senior management and developed a simple one-page intelligence report for the affiliates. Several meetings were held on the objectives of the program and the benefits to be derived from it. Within a thirty-day period, the research and development centers and the foreign affiliates began to transmit competitive information to the domestic planning department. The information was transmitted daily and incorporated into the planning process, as shown in Figure 9-1.

Phase II. Following six months of data transmission from the foreign affiliates, the planning staff recognized the need to expand the intelligence network in order to scan foreign publications for competitive intelligence.

Phase II involved a pilot program in which the information was received daily from various internal sources and an information supplier hired to scan foreign publications. The information supplier scanned and analyzed international information and distributed it to the corporate intelligence data base. In addition, the information supplier

Figure 9-1. Phase I of corporate intelligence network.

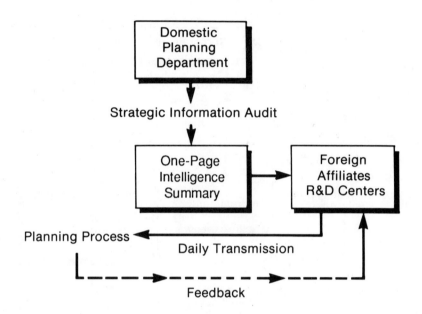

became actively involved in the feedback process (Figure 9-2).

Phase III. Phase III involved evaluating the effectiveness of the pilot program and the impact of the information on the strategic goals of the corporation.

Gathering of Foreign Published Intelligence

This task is one of the most difficult facing U.S. corporations. Although international data base publishers have done a superb job of developing data bases that report international news, few of these data bases scan, synthesize, and digest the international industry, market, and product publications. These publications, however, contain valuable product and market information not housed in international affiliates and R&D centers. The challenge remains how to efficiently capture this information on a timely basis.

One solution is to marshal the resources of overseas

Figure 9-2. Phase II of corporate intelligence network.

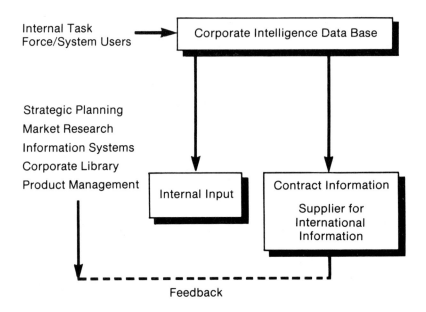

affiliates to scan, synthesize, and digest this information. Advantages to this approach include a more reliable translation of the language and a clearer understanding of the product and market information. Disadvantages might include the cost and the inability to obtain resource commitments from local affiliates.

Another solution is to contract with a firm that specializes in scanning and translating business periodicals for competitive activity. Advantages here are usually cost and objectivity. A possible disadvantage is a learning period needed by the outside firm to understand the focus of the scanning effort. Additionally, a legal contract must be drawn up between the information supplier and the company to ensure confidentiality of the effort. In some instances such a contract is necessary if the organization does not want the information supplier to resell the supplied information to another company or competitor.

Impact and Value of the Information

One method to use in evaluating the effectiveness of corporate intelligence networks is to answer the following questions within a year of setting up the network. Did any information uncovered in the tracking process enable us to

- Develop a new product?
- React quicker to a foreign competitor's erosion of our domestic market share?
- Reposition our products and promotion strategies abroad?
- Increase the profitability of our foreign brands?
- Anticipate specific competitors' new product development, pricing, or acquisition or diversification strategies?

If the answer is yes to one or more questions, the process is working and you can judge whether it has paid for itself.

Summary

With the accepted and widespread belief that there is no such thing as a U.S.-based company that is *solely* U.S.-based, the ability of an organization to gather intelligence on a global scale has been and will continue to be pivotal to long-term success. It can be postulated with a high degree of confidence that such an ability will make or break an organization.

10

Select Corporate Programs and Networks

"Strategy formation and competitive analysis go hand in hand. Neither has much without the other."

Sharon Whitfield, Vice-President Corporate Planning,
RJR Nabisco

No two corporations have developed the same "blueprint" for their corporate intelligence network. Although a methodology can be recommended for many companies, most corporations have to work around the culture of their organization. The business environment and the objectives of the organization (diversification, acquisitions, and so forth) have a significant impact on the content of the data base.

Actual cases from three leading U.S. corporations are presented in this chapter. The first, examining the activities of a leading pharmaceutical manufacturer, is important because of the present status of the pharmaceutical industry and the key strategic issues facing it. Additionally, this case also shows how corporations are using commercial on-line data bases as part of a corporate intelligence system.

The second case is about a financial institution and its development of a hard copy intelligence system. Although such systems are being widely supplanted by electronic or computerized information, hard copy systems will always be an effective way for distributing information to key decision makers.

The internal development of an electronic network that disseminates competitive information to company personnel globally is discussed in the third example. The corporation, a major hardware manufacturer and software vendor, has developed an electronic system that effectively integrates external and internal information sources. The system makes these sources available to any user on the network and can be searched via an interface that is simple to learn and use.

On-Line Access to Executive Decision Making

Joe Sonk, Director, Institutional Products, SquibbMark, a division of E. R. Squibb & Sons

Many executives today rely on traditional methods of research or on their staff although they could accelerate their access to information through simple methods of on-line searching. In spite of the inroads of electronic information technology, the notion still exists that "executives should not be sitting at terminals and typing—they should be making decisions." With the tools available today, however, there is no excuse for delaying executive decision making or action. Rapid access to on-line information enables the executive to search, download, and evaluate data for instant decision making. Those executives who make it their business to familiarize themselves with the information technology available could have a significant edge over their peers in competitive organizations.

Because of the competitive nature of the pharmaceutical industry and the key strategic issues facing it, such as cost containment issues and the tremendous influx of generic pharmaceuticals, strategic information must be current and made available immediately to decision makers. In the pharmaceutical industry, this requires a wide mix of internal and external information sources. Also, the pharmaceutical industry is very research-intensive, so the use of commercial data bases is a key element of strategic information. For instance, a number of commercial data bases provide information about patent filings, both in the United States and abroad. In the industry, information about patents is one of the most important external sources to tap on a systematic basis.

Accessing commercial data bases requires a learning curve and familiarity with the available information sources and data bases. With some simple search techniques, however, executives can pull up competitive company or product information, screen the contents for relevancy to the search, download the information to a personal computer, and integrate the information with the executive's own analysis (see Figure 10-1). In short, action is taken within minutes of receiving and analyzing the information. Oftentimes, the telephone is used to communicate the action or decision-making process.

A key example of the value of this rapid access to and evaluation of information occurred when a search of a specific company revealed cash flow problems. Through dissection of this company's financial reports, a competitor determined that the company would have significant problems in introducing a competitive drug. Evaluating up-to-

Figure 10-1.   Data base search and analysis.

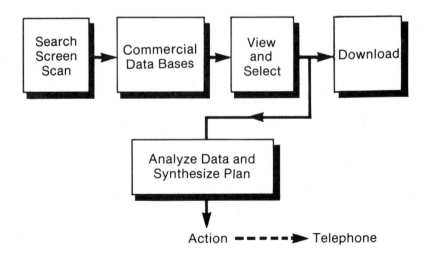

the-minute financial reports saved the competitor from waiting for detailed research reports either from its internal staffs or from external suppliers and resulted in effective decision making.

The situation becomes more complex with regard to international information. Here, the bottleneck lies in the translation of foreign publications. Services can be purchased, however, that rapidly translate this information. Knowledge of the foreign sources, however, is critical. The key here is that a process is necessary to automate the access of information so that decision making can be executed within minutes of gathering the information. In many organizations, this process has been automated through the development and installation of information systems that are "closer" to key decision makers. Examples of such systems are executive information systems and electronic mail systems that act as decision support systems for key decision makers.

How to Develop a Hard Copy System

M. C. Yocher, First Vice-President, People's Bank

Although the most efficient and clearly preferred approach to strategic intelligence is the use of an electronic system, this is not always possible, partly because of the lack of available integrated hardware and software and partly because of the rapid and dynamic changes both inside and outside the industry. Also, the complexity of the decision-making process is a major impediment to the use of electronic systems.

Consequently, hard copy for select information, whether from annual reports or other public information sources or simply computer printouts of strategic intelligence, is one of the more popular ways of disseminating information. Sources of information that can still be accessed in hard copy are shown in Table 10-1. Other hard copy information sources that are valuable include books,

Table 10-1.   Information accessible by hard copy.

Source	Strategic Information
Annual Report	Highlights goals, objectives, and strategies, and summarizes financial data (earnings, sales, and so forth).
10K/10Q	Provides detailed financial and other information about a company (for example, changes in company policy, stock ownership). Filed with the Securities and Exchange Commission, thus available to the public for viewing. Can be accessed via on-line commercial data bases.
Security Analyst Report	Companies purchase security analyst reports because many of them make accurate projections as to the future performance and profitability of corporations. These reports are valuable when a company systematically monitors its competitors. They are also valuable for investment purposes because they often detail information about a company's stock price. Some of these reports can be scanned rapidly through the use of commercial on-line data bases.
Industry Report	Published by many research firms that monitor markets within an industry. Oftentimes, such reports make a projection into the future (for example, sales of adjustable rate mortgages are expected to increase 15% by 1995).
FDIC Report	The FDIC publishes reports, newsletters, and other materials that monitor trends, government affairs, and other developments that affect the banking community.
Government Report	A number of branches of the federal government publish reports that are of interest to banks. One such branch is the Department of Commerce. Government reports at the state or city level may also contain valuable information.

Source	Strategic Information
Trade/Professional Journal	In the banking industry, many trade associations publish newsletters or magazines that report on activities that affect the industry. One such association is the American Banking Association, which publishes the *ABA Banking Journal*.

advertising and promotional material, and publications from consumer, recruiting, and consulting firms.

Hard copy, while currently being replaced by electronic information, will always form a part of strategic intelligence and will continue to be an effective medium for reaching a broad spectrum of decision makers. A selective process, however, must be used to prevent information abuse or information overload, such as the implementation of a strategic information audit. In addition, the audit, as discussed in Chapter 4, can effectively rate the utility of information sources, whether they are internal or external.

A library is also critical, as is a corporate mentality that does not encourage obsolete or useless intelligence. These remain key issues for the management information staff to seriously consider as paper and printing costs continue to escalate. Here, the trade-offs between hard copy and electronic information must carefully be weighed because abuse and overload can easily occur on electronic systems. This is a point that must be addressed when assessing the utility of internal and external information sources and when conducting a strategic information audit.

In the financial services industry, some firms evaluate a selective list of key traditional competitors as well as "trendsetters." The attempt is to focus on the dynamics and major changes in the industry and the implications for the organization today and in the future. A major environmental shift in the industry could cause a change in direction that could strengthen or weaken an organization. The consolidation in the industry demands an understanding of these shifts. However, it must be emphasized that hard copy should be used like a chart on a sailboat. It provides for a mapping of obstacles and possible routes, yet it must be evaluated against shifts in current, wind, and weather conditions as well as boat strengths, the shift being electronic information.

Finally, understanding the captain and crew or management of an organization is critical. This area is where hard copy is least valuable. The most useful source and interpretation of data is the people within the organization. This is the case in organizations that deal directly with customers or those that are constantly in contact with the external environment. Regardless of how information is collected or communicated, the quality of information can only be as good as the people who evaluate it.

In an industry environment where alliances or joint ventures between peers are growing, and complexity of change and its impact on business relationships is increasing, strategic intelligence must continue to be the concern of not only top management but also every employee. However, to become effective, the intelligence must be focused and managed so that decision makers can react to a dynamic and rapidly consolidating industry.

Information Access Services, Digital Equipment Corporation

Laura Hunt, Manager, Information Access Services

In 1984, the Market Information Services department of Digital Equipment Corporation began production of a major information systems effort designed to deliver competitive information to a worldwide sales and marketing audience and to showcase Digital networking technology and tools. The system was to contain full text documents from both internal and external information sources, be able to mail documents to any user on the network, and be searched via an easy-to-use interface that intermittent or novice users could easily learn.

The major task to be accomplished—distributing and

maintaining a large and complicated data base with daily updates—was made easier by the Digital videotex product, which enables the information provider to distribute a single data base to multiple users. VAX VTX was successfully married with the BASIS software from Information Dimensions, Inc. VTX/BASIS provided interesting infobase possibilities by combining powerful full text capabilities with the Digital front end to pass the user's interactive input through to the BASIS query functions. The resultant system offered a fine information-delivery vehicle with much potential.

The primary focus in the initial development was to build the technology to successfully accomplish the above. Little attention was paid to production and maintenance technology, including tools to update and modify the data base. Retrieval problems were also uncovered as users were added to the system. These problems represent a typical scenario when developing an information system: The system was designed by programming staff not involved with the information to be delivered, while the business professionals who had knowledge of system content were lacking understanding of how this information was to pass through the system to the user.

Development of a second infobase, using similar technology to the initial system, began in 1986. This data base was to contain industry- and account-based market information for Digital sales personnel working in specific industries. Concurrently, efforts were under way to provide an interactive user interface to commonly accessed statistical data bases used for market segmentation. Again, VAX VTX was selected as the delivery vehicle, with Digital's Relational Database product as the data base manager.

In 1986, the Information Access Services department of Market Information Services was formed to produce and maintain these data bases. The original staff was primarily concerned with content selection and acquisition, content analysis and abstracting, and thesaurus development for indexing and retrieval, with system support and development being handled by Digital information systems organizations. Additional staff was added as the systems were made more widely available to ensure the most timely delivery of the most relevant data, and to investigate broader possibilities for use and design of the data base.

The new staff was chosen on the basis of the varied skills needed to effectively deliver on-line strategic intelligence to the marketing and sales community. Information specialists with experience in data base production, those with understanding of programming and systems issues, and others with marketing experience were chosen to address system needs and promote system use and gather user data. With these backgrounds, the new staff recognized the potential inherent in the systems, and the need to approach content analysis, production, retrieval, and system development as an integrated effort.

After initial assessment, the new staff was able to prioritize system needs and map out a system strategy to address longer-term strategic goals. The first issues addressed were those that might increase use of the system: better retrieval and search response, easier user interface, and production system improvements that allowed more information to be added in a shorter amount of time. As a result of the changes made, usage was dramatically increased, allowing marketing personnel to gather significant user feedback to facilitate planning and further development.

The user feedback gathered revealed that infobase use at Digital is widespread and familiar to most employees; users, however, are not as a rule proficient in search methods, and are not happy with the prospect of diverse end-user systems that require separate training in order to achieve satisfactory search results. Most will not return to a system that seems hard to use and unresponsive, and will not use a system at all that seems to yield little result after time is spent to learn it. In addition, the proliferation of information sources and variance in availability and use of the systems made the need to look for marketing information in a number of places an increasing problem. Studies of users also revealed the need for even more market information to be delivered to an even broader audience.

The system strategy developed to address these findings was integration of data bases and the information contained within them to make retrieval easier for the user unfamiliar with individual data bases and allow different types of data to be retrieved with a single search statement or strategy. The strategy was designed to address the key factors of simplicity of use, complexity of data, and system flexibility and intelligence. The difficulties with linking preexisting data bases were partially overcome by creating a central thesaurus and indexing management system so that documents from different data bases could be classified in the same way for retrieval. This system allows key marketing concepts to be developed by use of a flexible, faceted indexing vocabulary that can be used in the creation of all systems. The system stands separately, on top of the individual data base management systems, to facilitate both indexing and user search and retrieval, without complete redesign of each separate system.

Other important components of the system strategy are designed to address technical advances in information management, including the integration of graphics and other image processing, windowing, hypertext, artificial intelligence, and natural language processing. Future development of the systems will follow the system strategy developed by a motivated, integrated staff of content, information, and system specialists whose primary goal is to bring traditional market research tools to the workstations of an ever-growing end-user audience of marketing and sales professionals. Future software products and development will be determined with input from both marketing and systems personnel, and will be based on user needs and expectations as analyzed from ongoing communication with end users.

There are no easy answers to these demands; there is no "quick and dirty" solution to the problem of delivering strategic information. But a system strategy developed and implemented by staff concerned with analyzing information content and viable technical alternatives to deliver this information can prevent inherent problems and ensure the flexibility and functionality necessary to develop the best solutions.

Summary

The three approaches discussed in this chapter demonstrate that corporate intelligence networks can vary between corporations. The approach described by Joe Sonk is unique because it applies the use of commercial data bases and incorporates this information with other sources, both internal and external. According to Sonk, those executives who make the effort to learn how to effectively use on-line systems have a "knowledge advantage" over their peers.

At People's Bank, a growing regional commercial bank, a hard copy approach to a corporate intelligence network works well within the company's culture, competitive environment, and budget. This approach underscores the fact that hard copy approaches will always be an integral part of strategic intelligence and an effective way of distributing information to decision makers. For Digital Equipment Corporation, the emphasis was to build technologies around a network and to create a separate department to produce and maintain the network.

11

Strategic Information Systems for Marketing

"Without new types of information that accurately depict competitive strategies before they unfold, marketplace opportunities as they occur, and competitive launches within a week of occurrence, great businesses with strong footholds and large market shares will be lost. We must be in front of competition with investments and innovations to build these new tools."

Jim Onalfo, Desserts Division Systems Manager,
General Foods USA

In many of today's corporations, a shared information network can come in textual or numeric form. Many networks that include both textual (for example, competitor tracking applications) and numeric data (such as market share) can become actionable marketing information data bases. Marketing information data bases have evolved over the last five years and represent a new type of information tool for the business community.

There are a number of reasons information data bases are becoming important marketing tools. Here are three major ones:

1. Competitive pressure has heightened dramatically, pushing management to search for new tools to track competition.
2. Top management has given clearer focus and direction and provided significantly increased funding to answer the questions:

187

- What is the competition doing?
- How is the competition doing?
- Where are the competition's weak spots?
- And how does all this relate to our business?

3. A new information glut has been created. The advent of scanner data combined with a shake-up in the syndicated information supplier industry has left companies scrambling for both survival and a market position.

Systems professionals have to become more innovative in developing new tools to track competition and improve decision making. Examples of these tools include market share and competitor tracking applications. These two applications are the most critical systems for marketing.

Market Share Applications (Numeric)

Marketing information assumed much greater usefulness with the computerization of data to help understand and track sales penetration in the marketplace. Initially, the information resulted from a single source, stand-alone SAMI data bases or stand-alone NIELSEN data bases. If the data were not available through a syndicated service, often self-generated data were created to assist market analysis. This may have been more expensive, but it served tracking purposes.

These were the first types of informational data bases to assist in tracking market results. They were considered revolutionary as a computer tool because of the extreme flexibility and speed they offered in reacting to the situations that occurred in the marketplace. These data often, however, reflected situations six to eight weeks after the data had been collected. In contrast, today it is possible to have data available in fewer than twenty days.

The second major improvement in collecting and manipulating marketing information, after computerization, was the development of integrated marketing data bases. A four-dimensional data base structure, which is a concept used to integrate information, is shown in Figure 11-1. This concept allows the following data to be combined:

- SAMI (retail warehouse withdrawal)
- NIELSEN (retail movement)
- Internal sales data
- Advertising effectiveness data
- Trade coupon evaluation
- Distribution effectiveness data

This information also has to be regularized on a consistent time basis (for example, weekly) and geography basis (usually regional)—a major challenge that, if not solved,

Figure 11-1.   Four-dimensional data base.

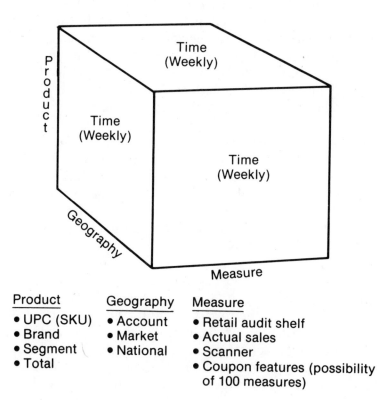

Product	Geography	Measure
• UPC (SKU)	• Account	• Retail audit shelf
• Brand	• Market	• Actual sales
• Segment	• National	• Scanner
• Total		• Coupon features (possibility of 100 measures)

will render an integrated data base ineffective. The four dimensions of the data base are product, geography, time, and measure.

The effectiveness of this type of information improves as managers learn more about how to use it. A key marketing executive stated that his company couldn't computerize marketing information because it was constantly fighting fires and situations that may occur once every three years. Naturally, the logical conclusion is that not much can be done to assist marketing. Well, that was the furthest thing from the truth. As a matter of fact, a clever solution to this problem was the use of fourth-generation languages. As it turned out, it was simple: Develop and install a flexible data base with reporting capabilities that allow the user to develop new reports as he needs them.

Two things happened when the flexible system was installed. First, the data base proved useful only with lower-level managers, who had the time to learn the first languages. Second, a large number of reports were stabilized, many more than anticipated. Only a few were "fire fighter" type reports, and flexibility reporting solved that need. It is often best in new and uncharted areas to just begin and let the users, supported by the technology, develop the systems over time.

Today, the ability of any executive to access information is greatly improved with icons (symbols of objects used as computer commands, rather than words). The main difference is that the icon is usually available on the computer monitor for the user to see or easily access. This "iconic" method usually lends itself to easier learning of computers. Also, new tools with easier access methods are being rapidly developed.

In spite of improved equipment, the critical problem top management will always have is "a lack of time," which will not allow them the luxury to sit at a terminal and deal with their information needs. It still remains primarily the work of staff members to access and decipher information to help answer questions asked by top management. Sophisticated tools will eventually allow rapid access and response of computer systems to management's questions.

Specifically, these are tools with "artificial intelligence" built into them. These tools look not only for positive or negative trends in large data bases but also for causes of the trends. This type of tool has selective problem-solving ability with logic built into it and quickly points out problems to management.

We are not there yet. The systems integration concept is shown in Figure 11-2. The strengths of the system are in the weekly structure of the data base, its hierarchy of account, market, and national data, and the flexibility of data access.

The type of system shown in Figure 11-2 directly helps to identify holes in the retail shelf that can be translated into sales opportunities. Other support tools are needed for the salespeople to assist their efforts to capture the sale.

In conjunction with new types of information tools, there are retail shelf condition applications. These are also tactical tools to help the sales force track conditions on the shelf (the number of facings, out-of-stock situations, point-of-sale pricing, special promotions, as well as activity of competitive products). The information can be available daily; however, the resources have to be in place to respond to the situations that occur. Figure 11-3 shows how a system concept can function. If implemented properly, the system can be very powerful support to the sales force.

The system shown in Figure 11-3 functions as follows:

- Data and questions are downloaded to the hand-held computer.
- The salesperson visits stores daily, scanning the shelves and collecting data to answer specific questions.
- At home, the salesperson sends data to the main computer and refreshes hand-held unit with new questions.
- System integrates data with other marketing systems.
- Next morning, on-shelf data are available to sales managers.

Figure 11-2. Integrated marketing information system.

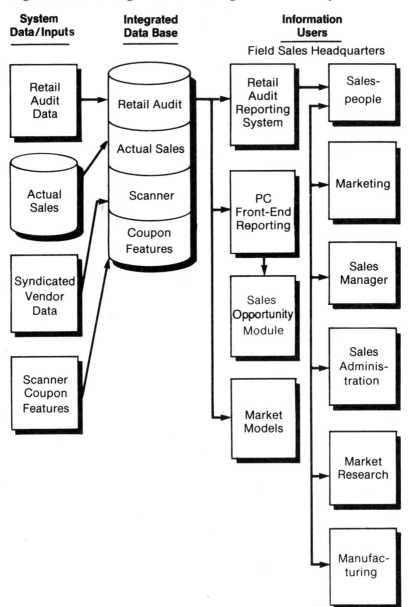

Figure 11-3. Retail shelf conditions flow.

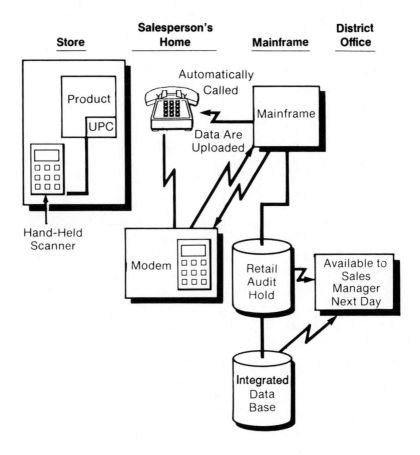

All the data bases and tools described will accumulate new data and information that can be used to present a very professional approach to servicing your customers and increasing sales. These tools, however, must be viewed as evolutionary and will constantly be changing as the business changes and the user finds the best way to use the tools. Therefore, management must fund not only the new development efforts but also any upgrading needed to cope with the changing dynamics of the business. Otherwise, these tools will become quickly obsolete.

The new wave of change facing marketing systems is the dramatic explosion of data coming from scanner technology. The impact of this new technology will affect much more than just the marketing applications. Also affected will be the organization, its managers, and other marketing-related activities. This new wave will create new types of decisions that need to be made, such as:

- Who decides what information to buy?
- How will it be delivered?
- How will it be used?
- Where will it be maintained?
- How will it be maintained?

Projections of the potential data that will be available show a growth fifty times current levels. For example, if one business has 500 million bytes of data showing monthly results today, this number jumps to 25 gigabytes with weekly scanner data. The exact size will depend on the number of measures needed and the amount of data purchased. The impact of such growth begs changes to today's practices. For example:

- The computer architecture becomes a key element in the equation of buying data. For example, personal computers are not designed for scanner volumes. How the data are to be processed, and where, are essential questions. Correct answers are vital to success, and the equipment decision cannot be left to individuals who do not understand the critical factor that must be known to correctly decide computer equipment configuration. Therefore, the computer architecture of the marketing and sales systems becomes even more significant because it is vital to the uses of scanner-produced information.
- The decision to buy syndicated data must now be performed at a high management level and must involve the top information system executive to en-

sure system compatibility and sufficient computer capacity to store scanner data. Advanced computer facilities planning is essential.

- Advance planning on how to use the data is essential. Mistakes here can be costly with so much data and cost involved. Today the information is bought with little concern about these considerations. This task becomes the most important task in the data purchasing decisions.
- Although the data need to be available on a more frequent time sequence, the massive amounts of scanner data will require new ways to deliver data to users. Thus, new data communications technology will be required.

Buying syndicated data like store-level scanner data without planning the type of computer could result in disaster and millions of dollars incorrectly spent. Likewise, response time could be too slow to be workable. The reliability of the system could be meaningless if the information is not responsive and useful.

The key steps to assist management in directing the marketing data base effort include a very detailed marketing information plan built from a strategic information plan for the entire business. The elements of a marketing information plan include:

- The development of scanner-based systems that integrate shipping data and SAMI warehouse withdrawal data
- The installation of personal computers on all marketing professionals' desks with basic word processing and spreadsheet tools
- Developing key accessing methods and reports to allow marketing professionals to use scanner data bases
- Developing a series of carefully built "prototype applications" to help management assess how to use

the information and understand what business reorganizations are necessary to take full advantage of scanner information. (For instance, as scanner systems get the user closer to the actual sale, marketing department structures are changing to look more like merchandising departments. The merchandising organizations will be more equipped to react to today's market situations than the traditional marketing organizations.)

- Building a road map of how other uses of scanner data can help other departments in the business. (For example, departments that plan production manufacturing schedules and departments that distribute product would like to have scanner data because it provides more detailed and up-to-date information to create and react to production schedules and sales shipments.)

Scanner information will have far-reaching effects on organizations and their structure in the future.

Competitive Intelligence Data Bases (Textual)

As previously discussed, text data base technology has evolved in the last two to three years, making it cost-effective to install textual bases on mainframes or on personal computers. The publishing industry has invested in computerizing textual information and thus many syndicated services have become available for accessing information on a "pay as you use" basis. Personal computers have also grown to the point where their use to access textual data has increased significantly.

Although the technical factor was important in the success of implementation, the most significant factor was the capability of an external business research firm that had perfected a process of scanning, clipping, organizing, synthesizing, and distributing relevant information focused against a specific business objective. The use of its process and skill mix proved to be essential to the implementation of this text-driven system.

The previous process was, at best, ad hoc and intermittently used. Competitive analysis reports were placed in various desks or files. It was not certain if all the "right" people read the material that was available to them. There was no structure or process in place to guarantee that this was happening. Consequently, a new approach was introduced—a textual competitive tracking system. The textual competitive tracking process provided a monthly data base, by brand and by competitor, showing all printed and published information. This meant that one did not have to subscribe to every periodical or magazine and read everything to ensure staying abreast of current happenings.

The implementation approach taken was a bottom–up technique. Each business was asked to review the idea and determine if the process made sense for it. After all agreed to the process, each business provided the strategy it wished pursued, and the search methodology was developed and implemented. Within three months the first issues were ready and distributed. Minor adjustments were instituted and provided in the next month's issues. Thereafter, monthly issues were consistently provided. The main objectives to keep in mind as the reports are issued are:

1. The document does not give answers to "what competition is doing," but rather provides additional pieces of information for business managers, who must sort through all relevant information and conclude what competition is doing. There is no system that will replace that task.
2. This type of decision support tool will evolve over time to a more complete application as managers realize how to take best advantage of it.

As each report is issued and situations are experienced, adjustments to the process can be made. For instance, as more and more competitors are tracked, as the business matures, and as product/marketing events change, a new search may be required for a different competitor or new sources tracked that clearly define competitor events. The most significant event will come from the integration of a textual delivery system with data-driven systems.

A flexible business focus is critical to this type of tool. For instance, as the business conditions change, search strategies must also change appropriately. The information must also be available for different methods of use—that is, hard copy reports to read at home or on planes, or on-line access for those who have personal computers.

A textual tool of this type is a unique application that requires very different skills not generally available in an organization and too costly to manage. This external information supplier brought the correct balance to allow a first-generation textual system implementation to competitive information computerization. It will be interesting to see how this type of tool evolves over time.

Summary

Critical marketing information systems have become vital business management tools. Their impact on business is significant in both tangible and intangible results. Market share and competitive action decisions are made from the information they supply. Marketing funding issues are also determined by analysis from marketing information systems. Also, and most recently, new sales have been directed through these systems. They have become tools that are truly business-building applications.

The results in the last five years have been significant, but very small compared with the benefits that are available. As we learn how to build artificial intelligence techniques into data analysis and provide useful direct input to top management, these benefits will multiply.

12

Tying the System to the Bottom Line

"In order to tie all systems to the bottom line, I use three sequential questions to guide any project's direction:
1. How much money is there to be made?
2. How much money is there to be made this year?
3. What is the amount?"

June R. Klein, Vice-President, Chase Manhattan Bank N.A.

There is no question that any investment in a corporate intelligence network must be tied to the bottom line. Whether the system increases productivity, adds value to the company's products and services, or enables the company to surpass the competition in a certain market, it must be tied to the bottom line. In this chapter specific corporations that have realized significant cost savings or revenue as a result of intelligence systems are examined.

Cost Savings

The strongest incentive for senior management to implement intelligence systems should be the success of other companies that have realized actual cost savings from these systems. A system developed for Citibank during 1985 is described in Chapter 5. According to Citibank:

The outcome is eye-opening. For less than $100,000 a year in operating costs, Citibank now has an informa-

199

tion distribution system that allows the firm's management to be strategically organized and see—then seize—opportunities.

Suppose you are in a product development group, with simple search routines, you can scan the database to see which new products the competition has come out with, and read analyses of how well these products are doing, how they're being promoted, and which demographic groups are responding best to them. That can help generate ideas for new Citibank services.

Citibank estimates that increased revenue attributable to Big Sister (the system's name) offsets the cost of running the system by as much as 20 times over.[1]

Internal Resources

Most companies pay close attention to their costs for consulting firms, information sources, and the internal staff required to handle information internally. Many corporations now hire external service companies to handle lower-value-added activities such as data gathering and collection and use their internal resources for higher levels of analysis. Figure 12-1 depicts the "value-added" chain of research and analysis for corporations.

Organizing information can account for nearly 35 to 40 percent of the cost of information research for a corporation. With today's tight budgets, firms are reluctant to spend $100,000 to $300,000 or more on research projects that are executed internally. As a result, they are looking to invest in their own internal intelligence networks as a resource for this research but are contracting with external companies for the lower-value-added activities of organizing information.

This "value-added" approach has raised productivity issues within organizations. Clearly, when two or more divisions hire independent research firms to execute the same project at hundreds of thousands of dollars, the issue

---

[1] "A Tale of Two Companies Coping With Information Overload." Reprinted from PC Week, June 21, 1988, pp. 59, 64. Copyright © 1988 Ziff Communications Company.

Figure 12-1. Value-added chain of information analysis.

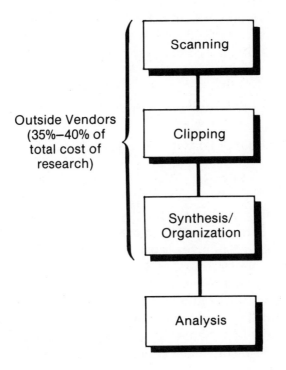

surfaces as to control and duplication of effort. Corporate intelligence networks attempt to minimize these issues.

Minimizing Duplication of Effort

The notion of minimizing duplication of effort has become a real problem in many corporations as it is directly correlated to productivity issues. The company's story that follows examines some of the costs that are associated with duplication of effort and suggests how to avoid it.

Determining the Cost of a Document

A major food company embarked on an effort to document the cost of generating internal projects or documents. To arrive at a dollar figure, it used the following formula:

$$\begin{array}{l} \text{Number of Hours} \quad \text{Manager's} \\ \qquad \text{to Produce} \quad \times \quad \text{Hourly} \quad + \\ \qquad \text{the Project} \qquad \text{Rate} \\[1em] \text{Out of Pocket} \qquad \text{Cost} \\ \qquad \text{Research and} \quad = \quad \text{of the} \\ \qquad \text{Materials Costs} \qquad \text{Document} \end{array}$$

With this formula, the results were staggering! For one department alone, projects and research reports represented nearly $2 million in actual cost to the corporation. Now, let us take this one step further. Generally, after a project or a research report has been completed, the findings from the report are summarized and presented to middle or senior management. The actual document is typically filed in a file drawer. More often than not, an issue from the initial report will resurface at some later time, or another division or staff group will embark on an effort to research the same issue. When this occurs, additional labor costs (time and materials) are spent. As a result, this cost of "reinventing the wheel" can cost corporations thousands and millions of dollars. The solution? Develop a system to catalog these documents and enable employees to access them on a worldwide basis.

White Collar Productivity: Saving Executive and Managerial Time

Many executives are faced with the challenge of "staying current" within an industry and informed of the competition without a large staff or even an assistant. As such, there is a tremendous amount of company and personal time spent on scanning and reading a wealth of literature. More importantly, even the "superhuman" executive finds it difficult to fit this task into a busy daily schedule. The time spent staying current costs the company money. The following is a study performed by Strategic Intelligence Systems, Inc., which surveyed clients on these issues.

A Survey of the Cost of Executive Activities

A series of executive activities that were being conducted in fifty Fortune 500 firms was reviewed.[2] For this study, "executive time" represents a fraction of total work time. This time includes activities that may not occur at the actual workplace (for example, commuting, work-related travel, preparing for work). Here are the findings regarding the amount of executive time spent on specific activities:

Executive Activities	Time Spent
Preparation for management meetings	
Preparation for ad hoc meetings	
Preparation of reports	60% professional time
Keeping abreast of the industry	
Information/analysis search for projects being considered	
Other professional activities	
(Assumption: equal weight for these executive activities)	
Letter preparation	
Article printing	
Telephone	20% professional time
Other nonprofessional activities	
Nonproductive activities	20% unproductive time

---

[2]Copyright Strategic Intelligence Systems, Inc., 1987.

If we assume that the average executive or manager attends one department meeting a month, the survey indicated that he or she spends approximately eighteen hours in preparation for this meeting. This time is broken down into the following tasks:

Activity	Time Spent
Gathering internal data for status reports	3.0 hours
Keeping abreast of the industry and the competition (scanning publications)	10.0 hours
Researching specific relevant information on new product development activity, industry trends, legal issues, acquisitions, and so on	5.0 hours
Total time spent in staying current with manual systems per month	18.0 hours
Total time spent in staying current with electronic systems per month	1.5 hours

Hypothetically, if it is assumed that a department consists of eight managers who are paid at an average rate of $25 per hour, the use of an electronic intelligence system could offer the following potential savings:

Total Manual Hours − Electronic Access Hours = Savings
18.0 hours   − 1.5 hours   = 16.5 hours/
                                                   month
                                                   savings

Savings of 16.5 hours/month @ $25/hour   = $412.50/
                                                   employee/
                                                   month
                                                   savings

Department of 8 employees = $3,300/
month
savings or
$39,600/
department a
year

In this model, if a company has ten departments with at least eight employees, the savings begin to add up to nearly $400,000. This figure becomes even higher with senior-level executives.

Examples: Methods for Controlling Costs of Intelligence Systems

Corporate intelligence systems do not have to be solely text-based systems. These systems can also utilize numeric data and offer significant savings to both a company and its customers. Following are five "real" examples of how these intelligence systems have been put to work in corporate settings and have resulted in significant cost savings.

Food Industry

Over the past few years, various product segments within the food industry have experienced tremendous consolidations, mergers, and acquisitions and reorganizations. This has been especially so in the confectionery industry, in which market share competition, both in the United States and abroad, has intensified. As such, the major players in the confectionery industry are looking to streamline their operations in an efficient manner that will result in cost savings and allow them to nurture their existing product lines or develop new ones.

One confectionery company, probably the largest in the world, realized such cost savings by forming an internal group that developed a shared information network on a global scale. The network became the corporation's information gold mine because it became the central depository for the following:

- Internal information sources
- External information sources
- Field intelligence

The key objective of this confectionery company was to minimize or eliminate duplication of effort in all three of these areas. Internal studies found that setting up a separate group within the corporation to develop the network, and thereby eliminating redundancies, inefficiencies, and duplication of effort, would result in an average annual cost savings of about $30 million over a five-year period.

In the past, various departments had purchased the same studies, contracted market research studies on the same topics, and hired consultants for similar purposes. The system worked to uncover these inefficiencies by consolidating information sources into a central depository.

Financial Services Industry

An intelligence network can realize revenue, not only cost savings, in the form of newly developed business. As the financial services industry continues to realize the effects of deregulation, financial institutions are relying on such networks to act as "early warning indicators" for new business that otherwise would not be sought.

For example, a major money center bank developed new business from a centralized information network that documented bids that were being taken for a direct payroll deposit system for a branch of the federal government. The revenues generated from this contract, which the bank had won, yielded an incremental $1 billion in new business. This new business more than offset the start-up costs and more than ten years of the operational costs of the network.

Consumer Packaged Goods

A data base that tracks textual material from published sources can provide insights about emerging growth markets, particularly in personal care and health care markets. Through its shared information network, a consumer packaged goods firm realized this and decided to develop a new and innovative mouthwash for the oral hygiene market.

This firm's data base highlighted and analyzed published sources. Another data base was designed that tracked consumer attitudes, product-driven trends, and technological developments in oral hygiene. That data base, sourced from secondary literature, abstracted articles and gave insightful analysis into developing trends.

Such analysis confirmed the market demand for oral hygiene products that were different from what was currently available to consumers. The product was subsequently rolled out to a national audience and the results were highly favorable, so much so that the company eventually was acquired by an organization that had the financial, marketing, and distribution resources to market this product on a global scale.

Diversified Manufacturer

A major manufacturer of glass, laboratory equipment, and optics developed an internal intelligence system after becoming increasingly concerned about inroads that a foreign competitor had made in the United States. This organization developed a corporatewide data base that could be searched by key word for either company information or product information of its major competitor.

In monitoring its competitor on a systematic basis, this manufacturer not only was able to track the activities of its competitors but also was able to diffuse the impact that select competitors were having on the organization's core domestic business by (1) making select tactical acquisitions in areas where its competitors were not strong and (2) developing strategic alliances with organizations to expand its international presence.

Thus, the internal intelligence network of this manufacturer resulted in tangible cost savings. Such a system underscores the significant inroads that foreign competitors are making in the United States and how the development of a shared information network can offset these inroads and affect the bottom line.

Pharmaceutical Industry

The pharmaceutical industry is a $25 billion business in which the major players compete on a global scale. The key strategic issues facing the industry, such as impending consolidation, cost containment factors, and reductions in research and development, have prompted top-level managers to set up an intelligence tracking system that efficiently monitors internal and external information sources and addresses tactical and strategic business problems.

The new business development department of a major pharmaceutical manufacturer developed an intelligence network that aids management in the following:

- Identifying new business opportunities that can be developed internally
- Making tactical or strategic acquisitions or developing research or licensing alliances
- Keeping abreast of patent filings and other research-intensive and product-driven activities in the industry

In one particular case, the manufacturer tapped the resources of an external information provider to gather information on a firm that the organization had sought to acquire. The information provider customized a competitor profile of the target company according to the specific specifications of the pharmaceutical firm. The report profiled the history of the acquisition candidate, the company's financial condition, and key products that it had introduced over the years. A key element in the production of this report was that the turnaround time was relatively brief, about ten days.

As it turned out, the research and analysis generated by this competitor profile saved millions of dollars for the pharmaceutical firm because the acquisition candidate was grossly overvalued. Thus, the competitor profile report resulted in cost savings for the new business development department by preventing it from overbidding for acquisitions.

Increased Revenue

Several companies have reported increased revenues as a direct result of the information contained in corporate intelligence networks.

> Big Sister has also helped the bank identify new opportunities. For one, articles in business and trade publications distributed over Big Sister alerted Citibank officials to more potential business in IRAs as tax shelters. Thus informed, Citibank quickly became one of the most aggressive marketers of IRAs. Similar articles also tipped bank officials to a growing consumer demand for mutual funds products. Again, the bank took quick action and saw its mutual funds business grow. And when the federal government said it would stop paying employees with paychecks and instead use direct deposit, Big Sister gave Citibank a three month jump on other banks to open new checking accounts for those federal workers.[3]

Jim Onalfo, Information Systems Manager for General Foods Corporation, states,

> It's dramatic what you can do with this type of database if you let your mind unravel. For instance, I have our weekly report on it, that is as leverageable as you can get. Data is transmitted over the database on Friday when it is processed. On Saturday, employees are churning through its impact, and on Monday morning we have the salesman running with it in the field. It's real world life. Sales have driven up because of it. Our salesmen are able to go out to the retailers with brand-spanking-new statistics each week and tell them in the most specific way that if you were selling our product instead of the competition, you would be realizing this much higher profit.[4]

---

[3]Reprinted from the April 27, 1988, issue of *The BusinessWeek Newsletter for Information Executives* by special permission, Copyright © 1988 by McGraw-Hill, Inc.

[4]"A Tale of Two Companies Coping With Information Overload." Reprinted from *PC Week*, June 21, 1988, pp. 59, 64. Copyright © 1988 Ziff Communications Company.

Summary

Corporations are realizing significant cost savings and executives are realizing time savings through the development of corporate intelligence networks. These networks allow decision makers to delegate the task of information retrieval to either an internal staff or an external organization and spend less time being information brokers and more time making decisions.

13

The Winners/The Losers

"Knowledge is of two kinds. We know a subject our-
selves, or we know where we can find information upon
it."

Samuel Johnson

The following company's story profiles a corporate information center at Kraft Foods, Inc.[1] This example was chosen
for the final chapter for several reasons, including the following:

- Kraft used a smart business approach to an information network.
- The information network at Kraft uses the resources
  of several departments.
- The network addresses the appropriate mix of today's
  tactical questions and tomorrow's strategic questions.
- The network has the utmost support from senior
  management.

Winning at the Information Game:
A Marketing Research Perspective

The primary goal of business today is to win in the
marketplace. Winning means prosperity for the company
and career success for the individual.

---

[1]The Kraft Foods, Inc. story originally appeared in *Information Management Review*, vol. 4, no. 1 (Summer 1988). It is adapted with the permission of Aspen Publishers, Inc., © 1988.

The best way to win is to take a business approach in all your activities. Although the focus here is on taking a business approach to marketing research, the same winning concepts and principles can be transferred to any segment of the information industry. The major question you should ask is, How can I take more of a business approach to my job and my industry? The benefit of asking this question is to put you closer to winning at the information game!

In this example the following topics are discussed:

- Taking a business approach
- Kraft marketing information department's (KMID) situation
- Performance criteria and ways to influence performance
- Case study on development of the corporate marketing information center (CMIC), a division within KMID

Taking a Business Approach. The way to take a business approach to your job and industry is to develop a goal and operating style that are synonymous with your management. Management's goal is to be first in the marketplace. The advantages of being first are typically higher company profits, market strength, and flexibility. A convenient way of keeping the goal of being first on your mind is to use FIRST as a convenient acronym to define a winning operating style:

- Facts
- Innovation
- Risk
- Smart business decisions
- Time and events schedules

The FIRST operating style (see Table 13-1) involves (1) clarifying the facts surrounding the situation, (2) searching for ways to improve performance and beat competition via innovation, (3) accepting personal risk in selling programs

Table 13-1. FIRST operating style.

Decision-Making Style	Key Directives
■ Facts	■ Know strengths and weaknesses ■ Know competition and end users
■ Innovation	■ Examine new approaches and options ■ Hire and leverage the best
■ Risk acceptance	■ Sell ideas to management
■ Smart business decisions	■ Consider and involve management
■ Time and events schedules	■ Use project management approach

to management, (4) ensuring smart decisions are made that will stand up to close business scrutiny, and (5) delivering on a time and events schedule as promised.

The major benefit of using the FIRST operating style is that it enables you to

- Meet user and management needs
- Create an information edge over competition
- Innovate and implement successfully

The CMIC case demonstrates how this FIRST operating style is put into practice. However, a general understanding of KMID's situation is important before reviewing the case.

Kraft Marketing Information Department. To provide context, KMID is similar to many large marketing research departments in the consumer packaged goods industry, such as those of General Foods, Quaker Oats, and General Mills. KMID also operates like many other businesses in the information industry. It is a service organization dedicated to answering clients' questions and solving their problems. This involves helping anyone in Kraft with a marketing question. The primary clients are marketing, management, planners, and research and development personnel.

Figure 13-1 highlights the major areas KMID manages, namely:

- Client questions at Kraft
- KMID operations, composed of information, staff, and technical facilities
- General environment, consisting of consumers, information providers, and technology

Figure 13-1.   What does KMID manage?

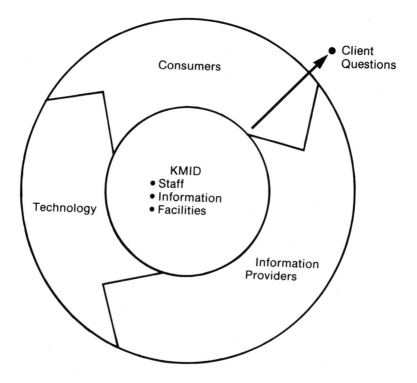

The types of client questions KMID fields can be seg-mented according to short-term and long-term objectives and goals. The short-term questions focus on specific ele-ments of the marketing mix, including the so-called four Ps: price, product, promotion, and placement. Typically, KMID answers questions on the following topics:

- *Pricing.* Can we anticipate competitive pricing moves?
- *Product.* Should we develop line extensions?
- *Promotion.* Should we offer special trade promotions to build end-aisle displays at retail outlets?
- *Placement.* Are we losing distribution to a new com-petitive product offering?

As Figure 13-2 shows, KMID also looks to answer questions that are long-term in scope. These tend to be broad and strategic questions that help Kraft understand its markets, customers, and competitors. The questions may include research allocation, major product introductions, and acquisitions.

Figure 13-2. What questions do clients ask?

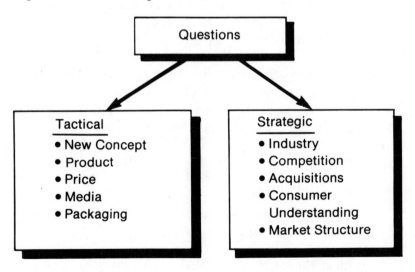

KMID's objective is to address the right mix of tactical and strategic questions to help Kraft win in the marketplace. KMID answers client questions through managing a mix of primary, syndicated, and secondary information consisting of consumer surveys and sales and public data.

The majority of KMID staff are research analyst's functioning as account executives by integrating primary and secondary data to address client questions. The analysts are supported by technical specialists who provide information services in the form of a corporate marketing information center. Essentially, analysts work on the development and evaluation of major programs, such as advertising campaigns, new products, and promotional strategies.

The role of the technical specialist is to make the analyst's or client's job easier by providing information management, systems, data bases, and analytic support. KMID's organizational structure (like that of many large marketing research departments) is analogous to that of an ad agency with its account management team supported by functional experts (media, research, and so on).

Technical specialists tend to differ from analysts in that they do not develop or evaluate the program. Typically, they have expertise in support functional areas such as syndicated or secondary information or in analysis of information that is statistical in nature.

Performance Criteria and Ways to Influence Performance. KMID receives its "report card" from management and direct users at Kraft. These two groups judge KMID by the same criteria as they judge themselves. KMID must

- Help the business with its information and goals (for example, increased market share, market growth, and increased profits)
- Deliver more, better, faster, and less expensive services than the competition

To meet these criteria, KMID has to make smart business decisions about

- What information is purchased
- How the information is purchased
- How the information is analyzed
- What and how outside support is used
- What staff is hired and how they are trained
- What facilities and technology are purchased or leased

Generally, the considerations that apply to these questions include the following:

- The importance of the information
- The amount of analysis required to answer the question
- Ease of use
- Willingness of the client to pay
- Timing
- Relative value vis-à-vis other options
- Potential for any competitive advantage

Many of the preceding considerations also involve critical "make" (develop internally) versus "buy" (acquire externally) decisions. Marketing research must frequently choose between commissioning a proprietary consumer survey (make) or purchasing syndicated information (buy), developing in-house staff (make) or hiring outside experts (buy), and processing information internally (make) or engaging in a time-share arrangement with an outside supplier (buy).

Aside from the make versus buy decision, the performance criteria listed above should be used to make other decisions. Table 13-1 also lists some key directives that should be kept in mind when using this approach. What this system does is force marketing research to view itself as a business within a business. Each major program should be evaluated on how it can realistically (on the basis of facts) be used to help the business and enhance its competitive position. An effort should be made to look at all options (no matter how different they are from the norm) to see if a better "mousetrap" can be built.

Another objective is to view the project from management's perspective to make sure that they buy into the proposition that this will positively influence the business thinking behind the program. A project management approach ensures that you have considered all the major program elements and their proper sequence to develop realistic completion dates. This increases the likelihood that the program will be delivered as promised.

Development of the Corporate Marketing Information Center. KMID first started thinking about building an information center after auditing the department for competitive strengths and weaknesses. KMID felt that the absence of an information center was a major problem and barrier to effectiveness and efficiency. As a result, the department decided to do its homework and check its competitive position.

KMID conducted competitive intelligence by surveying major food companies' information centers. Following is a profile of Kraft's most advanced competitor's information center. As you can see, the center is very developed in terms of organizing and networking information via a central facility, contracts, staff, and data bases.

- Eight professionals at corporate headquarters
- 2,500-square-foot facility
- Computer and retrieval equipment
- Common information contracts
- Computer network with division centers (seventeen people)
- On-line abstracts of reports (10,000 +)

KMID reviewed the situation with upper management and articulated the problems caused by the absence of a center. These centered on a lack of organization (limited use of library science techniques), inefficient manual rather than computer-aided processes being used, and little information sharing across divisions. This caused client frustrations in obtaining needed information and put Kraft at an information disadvantage versus some sophisticated food companies.

KMID further sold management on the concept and benefits of a corporate marketing information center. CMICs provide more, better, faster, and less expensive information to clients for use in decision making. Specific benefits are:

Better Quality of Business Intelligence

More comprehensive (internal and external information)
More integrated (networking)
Fewer information gaps (new information)

Cost and Timing Efficiencies

Reuse information and reduce overlaps
Save clients time and money

Management endorsed the information center concept and also agreed with two KMID recommendations for designing and implementing the center:

1. Use an outside consultant to assist in all project phases.
2. Survey clients to ensure the center's design fits their needs.

KMID designed the CMIC with the goal of giving the right information to the right person at the right time. This called for:

- Creating a central facility where clients could go for information
- Answering clients' easy questions via a phone hotline service
- Answering clients' complex questions via an in-depth consulting service
- Ensuring that clients received the needed informa-

tion and copies via efficient access tools and equipment

- Putting much of KMID's information on a data base so that past projects could be retrieved and suppliers' timing and cost performance monitored
- Creating an internal communications program with presentations, brochures, and internal seminars to generate client usage of the network

Upon receiving management design approval, the center went from ground zero (no staff, facility, or equipment) to being operational in six months. The principal reasons that implementation was achieved this fast are that KMID

- Targeted services to core users
- Designed and followed a tough time and events schedule
- Hired experienced and computer-proficient staff members
- Leveraged outside suppliers for data bases and manpower needs

KMID has further improved client service and increased operating efficiencies by

- Merging the CMIC with another internal business information center to broaden joint information capabilities
- Networking Kraft divisional marketing research departments and CMIC's on-line data bases of research reports
- Closing new product information gaps by working closely with an outside supplier

All these efficiencies notwithstanding, there are numerous opportunities to further improve performance by integrating and simplifying data bases, work processes, and products and services. The primary strategy to realize these opportunities will be to focus on strategic partnerships with selected suppliers. This will give KMID access to needed information and evolving technology.

Summary

The downside of not taking a business approach is perilous. Warning symptoms of impending disaster are

- Tactical approach is more dominant than the strategic.
- New information sources and technologies are neglected.
- Information facilities are developed with blind spots.
- Outside resources are not fully leveraged.

These conditions create inefficiencies, competitive disadvantages, and low morale in the organization. Inevitably, management intervenes and cleans house by removing poor performers and unnecessary overhead. This has happened to several marketing research departments in the last five years. It means the department lost control and credibility, which constitutes losing in every sense of the word.

You can avoid such a situation and win at the information game by using a business approach. It all starts with asking that simple question, How can I take a more businesslike approach to my job and industry?

Afterword

The examples and principles described in this book have been directed toward communicating the benefits of a corporate intelligence network. These systems are successful when they affect the day-to-day operations of the organization.

The central issues in the book not only mirror the critical stages of developing a shared intelligence network but also represent the major responsibilities of top management, the internal champion, the task force, and others involved in implementing the network. This process is summarized in Appendix L.

The development of centralized information networks has been evolving during the past five years. The corporations cited in this book have taken a leadership role in the development of these systems. Others have followed similar paths. Corporate intelligence networks are currently "the next step" and will be aided by sophisticated artificial intelligence techniques as we enter the next century. Because these networks take at least five years to evolve, those companies that initiate systems soon will have a head start on their competition. Organizations will continue to seek to reduce their information overload. During the 1990s and into the twenty-first century, there will be a goal of "information downsizing" to achieve higher-value analytical information on a "real time" basis. This goal is for the "intelligent corporation."

Appendix A
Industry Trends

FINANCIAL SERVICES INDUSTRY

Consumer rates have declined sharply since the June 5, 1989, prime rate cut by major banks. Many lenders have reduced their fixed mortgage rates below 10 percent, as CD, MMA, and consumer credit rates also decline.

- *Bank Rate Monitor* suggests that the accelerated pace at which consumer rates declined in the week following the prime rate cut indicates the beginning of a downward cycle.
- A reduction in inflationary pressure and a spate of economic reports that showed the economy to be slowing have allowed the Fed to reduce short-term rates for the first time since February 1987. Banks responded by cutting their prime lending rate, after six consecutive increases.
- Major banks reduced their one-year CD rate by as much as 0.5 percent in the week following the prime rate move. Adjustable rate loans will be affected by the prime rate cut, since many of these vehicles are tied to the prime.
- The decline in rates has allowed such major mortgage lenders as Sears to reduce their fixed mortgage rates below 10 percent. Sears is currently charging 9.675 percent (with a charge of two points) for its thirty-year vehicle. Sears Mortgage reported a 50 percent surge in originations over the past several months thanks to the lower mortgage rates.

IMPLICATIONS: The move toward lower rates may be complicated by the 0.9 percent surge in the May wholesale inflation rate. However, the continued advance in dollar price may cause the Fed to directly intervene in the market with a discount rate cut.

Appendixes A through G represent a series of abstracts that are examples of organized and analyzed information from external sources. These abstracts encompass various topic areas that are mentioned in the text and are typically used to effectively segment information for searching and retrieval purposes.

REFERENCES: 1. "Downcycle May Be Under Way," *Bank Rate Monitor,*
June 12, 1989, pp. 1, 4.
2. "Mortgage Rate Drop Heats Up Housing Market,"
USA Today, June 13, 1989, p. B1.

KEY WORDS: Interest Rates

AUTOMOTIVE INDUSTRY

Falling new car sales and higher marketing costs are expected to
translate into lower profits for the Big 3 U.S. automakers this year.

- Initially, many forecasts called for 1989 new car and truck sales
  to fall about 500,000 below last year's strong showing of 15.8
  million.
- GM Chairman Roger Smith expects sales to fall to about 15
  million.
- In addition to economic uncertainties, higher interest rates, a
  saturated market, and higher auto prices, other factors are
  involved in declining sales.
- According to the so-called multiplier effect, each job in an auto
  assembly plant generates five to eight additional jobs elsewhere. However, with sharp declines in production, the impact
  of the downturn in sales will be more severe on a regional
  basis.

IMPLICATIONS: Any downturn will also affect everyone from brake
manufacturers to steel suppliers, as well as organizations that have
automakers as key service clients (computer firms, engineers, and so
on).

REFERENCES: 1. "Auto Slump Could Send Tremors Through Softening
U.S. Economy," *Investor's Daily,* June 9, 1989, p. 32.
2. "Dark Clouds Gather Over Sated Car Market," *Investor's Daily,* June 9, 1989, pp. 1, 32.

KEY WORDS: Smith, GM

Appendix B

Environmental Trends

AUTOMOTIVE INDUSTRY

The Environmental Protection Agency (EPA) is asking President Bush to support mandatory requirements for the use of cars and buses that use fuel other than gasoline.

- To date, the idea has been met with stiff opposition.
- A prototype bill features proposals favored by the EPA to require 50 percent of new cars and buses in the twenty-five most polluted U.S. cities to run on methanol, ethanol, or compressed natural gas beginning in 1995.
- Henson Moore, a deputy secretary with the Department of Energy, is against this requirement, claiming that the economic costs would be higher than the EPA estimates.
- Automakers and the oil industries oppose any requirement for fuel switching. They cite problems with methanol. The American Petroleum Institute warns that it would cost $18 billion to $24 billion to build about sixty new methanol plants to supply fuel under the EPA proposal.
- In addition, energy industry analysts note that extra natural gas needed to make the methanol would have to be imported from the Middle East, posing the same national security threat as imported oil.

IMPLICATIONS: The prospects of pressures for manufacturers to produce vehicles that use alternative fuels may represent the most sweeping changes in the history of automobile and petroleum industries.

REFERENCES: 1. "Clean Air Costly, Automakers Say," *Washington Post,* June 14, 1989, p. F1.
2. "Carmakers Pressed to Radically Re-Engineer Autos," *Investor's Daily,* June 29, 1989, p. 31.

KEY WORDS: EPA, Bush, Department of Energy

CHEMICAL INDUSTRY

At a meeting of the United Nations Environment Program in Helsinki, eighty countries signed a declaration to stop all production and consumption of chlorofluorocarbons (CFCs), which damage the ozone layer, by the year 2000. The eighty nations also supported establishment of a global fund that would aid Third World nations in developing alternatives to CFCs.

IMPLICATIONS: Manufacturers should begin to search for a solution to the CFC problem before they find their products banned in many nations. Sales are bound to drop dramatically if bans are placed into effect.

REFERENCES: 1."Eighty Countries Support CFC Ban," *Chemicalweek,* May 10, 1989, p. 16.
2. "EC Ministers Agree to Ban CFCs by 2000," *HAPPI,* April 1989, p. 10.

KEY WORDS: United Nations Environment Program, Helsinki, CFC

FOOD INDUSTRY

Consumer activists at a House hearing called for tougher laws against pesticide residues in food and suggested that Congress ban the use of any pesticide that could cause cancer.

- Agricultural groups complained that the "negligible risk" standard proposed in a House bill is too extreme because it does not take into account the benefits of chemical use, without which food production would suffer.
- The "negligible risk" bill, sponsored by Rep. Henry Waxman, would bar the use of chemicals if they carried a risk of one cancer case per one million people.
- A poll by the Food Marketing Institute showed consumer confidence was shaken by the scares over the tampering with Chilean grapes and the possible health effects from Alar, which regulates the color and firmness of apples.
- Representatives of the Natural Resources Defense Fund, Public Citizen, and the Public Interest Research Group said that no cancer-causing chemicals should be allowed in agricultural use at all.

- The agricultural groups said that the economic benefits of farm chemicals should be taken into account. The bill could block the use of fumigants needed to keep grain in top condition and prevent infestation by crop pests.

IMPLICATIONS: Stiffer but realistic pesticide laws should be proposed to Congress. Although agricultural groups may suffer economically from chemical restrictions, this minimal loss cannot compare with the health hazard chemicals pose to the population, not to mention the drop in sales for specific food products due to a poison scare. In addition, chemical manufacturers should attempt to find safer products without compromising effectiveness.

REFERENCES: 1. "Consumers Call for Stiffer Pesticide Law," *Investor's Daily*, June 11, 1989, p. 13.
2. "Alar Campaign Steps Up," *Chemical Marketing Reporter*, May 15, 1989, pp. 7, 12.
3. "The Pesticide Scare: Changing Public Perception," *Chemical Week*, May 2, 1989, pp. 28–30.

KEY WORDS: Congress, Rep. Henry Waxman, Food Marketing Institute, Alar, Natural Resources Defense Fund, Public Citizen, Public Interest Research Group

Appendix C

Legislation

The Federal Reserve has expanded banks' securities powers to include corporate debt underwriting. The central bank applied several restrictions and limitations to this ruling. Many in Congress vocally opposed the ruling, which will allow banks to underwrite speculative debt, citing the mounting volume of LBO debt held by commercial banks and the S&L crisis—which many lawmakers argued grew out of the deregulation of the thrift industry.

- According to executives quoted in the *American Banker*, major banks plan to quickly enter the corporate debt markets.
- The Fed previously ruled that banks could underwrite commercial paper, mortgage-backed securities, municipal bonds, and several other types of collateralized issues in 1987.
- The latest ruling applies the same restrictions that were placed under these previous rulings. These limitations include:
  1. Underwriting must be conducted through a separate subsidiary of the bank's holding company.
  2. Revenue derived from underwriting must not exceed 5 percent of the unit's total revenue.
- The ruling grew out of requests from five major banks: Citicorp, Chase, J. P. Morgan, Bankers Trust, and Security Pacific.
- Banks that plan to exercise corporate debt underwriting powers must submit a proposal outlining how the bank will capitalize underwriting subsidiaries in order to assure that the capital of the bank holding company will not be depleted.
- In an important contingent to the ruling, the Fed cleared the way for banks to enter the equities underwriting market in one year. The one-year period is designed to allow Congress an opportunity to enact legislation covering various underwriting issues.

REFERENCES: 1. "Fed Moves to Allow Banks to Underwrite Corporate Debt; Equity Powers Withheld," P. Duke, *The Wall Street Journal*, January 19, 1989, pp. A3, A4.

2. "Banks Get Nod on Corporate Debt," *American Banker,* January 19, 1989, pp. 1, 16.

KEY WORDS: Federal Reserve, Corporate Debt Underwriting

AUTOMOTIVE INDUSTRY

The NHTSA will require rear-seat lap and shoulder belts in new passenger cars, effective January 1990.

- According to the agency, 16 percent of all rear-seat passengers currently use the lap safety belts. The agency maintains that if this level were 100 percent, six hundred additional lives would be saved.
- The regulation is not expected to have a negative effect on U.S. automakers, who already planned to make shoulder belts standard for rear-seat passengers in 1990 models. The foreign automakers will be saddled with most of these costs.
- The rule applies to all new passenger cars except convertibles. Vans, utility vehicles, and light trucks are exempt from the regulation, but the NHTSA said it is investigating whether to extend the rule to cover those vehicles.

REFERENCES: 1. "Rear-Seat Shoulder Belts Are Ordered for New Cars," *The Wall Street Journal,* June 13, 1989, p. C19.
2. "New Rule Requires Belts in Back Seats of 1990-Model Cars," *The New York Times,* June 15, 1989, p. A24.

KEY WORDS: NHTSA

CHEMICAL/DETERGENT INDUSTRIES

The future of sodium tripolyphosphate (STPP) is cloudy as legislation ponders its use in heavy-duty laundry detergents. Eroding demand, offset to some degree by the success of new powder/bleach formulations, is expected to continue throughout 1989, as bans in Ohio and Pennsylvania take effect the first of next year.

- Legislation is also pending in Georgia, South Carolina, Idaho, and Oregon. Lewis Furman, director of marketing for the phosphorus division at FMC Corporation, says the threat of bans

exists in nearly ten states and asserts that producers will begin
to question the benefit of powders with STPP.

■ The introduction of Tide With Bleach and testing of Clorox Super
Detergent helped the powder market by taking from liquids.
Liquids are growing at a much slower rate than in past years.

IMPLICATIONS: Manufacturers of products containing STPP would be
wise to consider different formulations excluding this chemical. Though
bans are currently on a limited basis, nationwide publicity of this issue
could generate undesired repercussions. In addition, the chemical may
become difficult to attain and manufacturers will be unable to purchase needed quantities.

REFERENCES: 1. "STPP Producers Brood Over Phosphate Bans," Chemical Marketing Reporter, May 1, 1989, p. 33.
2. "Henkel Moves to P-Free Detergents," HAPPI, June
1989, p. 24.

KEY WORDS: STPP, Tide With Bleach, Super Detergent, Clorox, FMC
Corporation, Lewis Furman

Phosphorus producers are considering the pitfalls of investing too much
of their product in the heavy-duty laundry detergent market. Although
companies will continue to fight legislation, it is inevitable that the
trend toward enacting bans will also continue, according to a business
director for phosphorus and derivatives at Monsanto Chemical Company.

■ During a press briefing, Monsanto executives pointed out that
only 3 percent of the phosphorus buildup in the nation's rivers,
lakes, and streams is contributed by detergent phosphates. The
remaining 97 percent emanates primarily from animal and
human waste and agricultural runoff.

■ The alternative that producers such as Monsanto have arrived
at is not total defeat, but rather a gradual movement away
from phosphorus production for use in detergents. This means
putting roughly one-third of its phosphorus into areas such as
food, intermediates, and industrial and institutional cleaning.

■ The director of marketing for the phosphorus division at FMC
Corporation projects that U.S. demand for phosphates over the
next three years will be flat and will most likely decline by 5
percent or more.

IMPLICATIONS: It is understandable that phosphorus producers would oppose a ban on phosphorus use in detergents. However, if it is true that 97 percent of the buildup derives from the sources mentioned, such a ban on detergents alone would, in effect, be futile. Sewage treatment methods and farming chemicals need to be evaluated in tandem with phosphate use in detergents.

REFERENCES: 1. STPP Producers Prepare for the Inevitable," *Chemical Marketing Reporter*, May 29, 1989, p. 23.
2. "FMC Reduces STPP Pricing," *Chemical Marketing Reporter*, August 7, 1989, p. 27.

KEY WORDS: Monsanto Chemical Company, FMC Corporation, Phosphorus

PHARMACEUTICAL INDUSTRY

The FDA has approved use of a genetically engineered drug that can help reduce anemia in patients suffering from kidney failure. Developed under the agency's orphan drug program, erythropoietin (EPO) will be marketed by Amgen, Inc. under the trade name Epogen.

- Amgen becomes the second biotechnological company to market a major drug, after Genentech, Inc. The company will be allowed to market the drug immediately.
- The cost of EPO is $4,000 to $6,000 per patient annually. It is expected that patients will receive government assistance.
- The FDA approval, however, appears to complicate Amgen's ongoing dispute with Johnson & Johnson. Amgen is licensed to sell EPO for dialysis patients in the United States, but J&J has all rights elsewhere and rights for other indications in the United States.
- J&J filed suit against Amgen claiming that the company has reneged on its responsibility to submit predialysis clinical data in its FDA application.
- Although Amgen salespeople cannot promote EPO for nondialysis use, doctors will be allowed to prescribe it as they wish.
- A J&J spokesman said Ortho will start marketing EPO when the dispute with Amgen is settled. J&J still hopes that Amgen will supply the drug, although its own plants could produce it. The FDA has yet to approve labeling for Ortho's version of EPO, called Eprex.

- Amgen's EPO sales are still potentially threatened by the company's patent dispute with Genetics Institute, which holds competing patent rights.

IMPLICATIONS: It is important that these companies resolve their disputes as soon as possible because although they apparently have time to spare, kidney failure patients do not. EPO would allow patients to live a more normal life. Constant dialysis treatments and frequent transfusions drain the blood of necessary nutrients and minerals. Because EPO stimulates the growth of red blood cells, more oxygen can be transported throughout the body.

REFERENCES: 1. "Anemia Drug Okayed," *Chemical Marketing Reporter*, June 5, 1989, p. 7.
2. "FDA Approves Amgen's New Biotech Drug," *Investor's Daily*, June 2, 1989, pp. 1, 30.

KEY WORDS: FDA, EPO, Amgen, Inc., Epogen, J&J, Eprex

Appendix D
Competitor Activity

AUTOMOTIVE INDUSTRY

GM will give its "big car" manufacturing group responsibility for all of the company's domestic small-car production. This is a shift that reverses a major goal of GM's massive reorganization plan of 1984.

- Clearly, the idea of this is to realize further cost savings.
- As per this new strategy, the engineering and manufacturing of the compact cars (Chevrolet-Pontiac-GM of Canada) are being transferred to the big-car group (Buick-Oldsmobile-Cadillac).
- The big-car group already controls production of GM's other two compact car lines (the J and N body cars).
- The idea behind the shift is that it will make it easier for GM to carry out plans to merge the three separate small-car platforms into one small-car platform that can share common parts and allow production of several different models in a single plant.

IMPLICATIONS: Although the decision makes sense on the basis of cost, the decision to consolidate these functions may baffle some observers. For one, the Buick-Olds-Cadillac group consists of decentralized units that already have increased quality and have cut costs better than the centralized small-car group (Chevrolet-Pontiac-Canada operation).

REFERENCES: 1. "GM to Consolidate Big, Small Car Roles for Cost Savings, Reversing Revamp Goal," *The Wall Street Journal,* June 7, 1989, p. A4.
2. "GM Sets a Major Realignment," *The New York Times,* June 7, 1989, p. D4.

KEY WORDS: GM, Chevrolet, Pontiac, Oldsmobile, Cadillac

Tenneco will restructure its automotive parts unit, including the sale of its automotive retail division and the acquisition of a Georgia brake manufacturing plant.

- The restructuring is designed to strengthen Tenneco's presence in the parts business.

- Under the plan, Tenneco Automotive will sell its retail division (Toronto) to a group of Canadian investors led by Stanley Goldfarb and Fred Karp, chair of Speedy King Muffler.
- The divested unit, which accounted for $260 million of the automotive division's $1.7 billion in sales revenues, operates 709 muffler shops in five countries.
- The automotive division, which accounts for about 21 percent of Tenneco's earnings, is one of the corporation's most profitable and includes the Monroe Auto Equipment Company. Monroe manufactures more than 50 percent of the shock absorbers made in the United States.
- Tenneco has also completed the acquisition of a nonasbestos brake manufacturing plant in Cartersville, Georgia, from Inter-friction USA for an undisclosed sum.

IMPLICATIONS: As vertically integrated as Tenneco is, the company is looking to streamline its automotive division and redeploy capital in automotive markets that are growing and less dependent on shifts in the economy.

REFERENCES: 1. "Tenneco Revamping Auto Parts Subsidiary," *Investor's Daily*, June 13, 1989, p. 8.
2. "Tenneco to Reorganize Auto Parts Business," *The New York Times*, June 13, 1989, p. D5.

KEY WORDS: Tenneco

PACKAGING/DETERGENT INDUSTRIES

Procter & Gamble, in conjunction with some of its packaging suppliers, has unveiled new plastic packaging for some of its detergent products that will aid in the nation's solid waste disposal efforts.

- Bottles of Downy fabric softener, Liquid Tide, and Liquid Cheer will now be made from 20 to 30 percent recycled high-density polyethylene (HDPE). The three-layer bottles made by Plastipak Packaging, Inc. incorporate scrap HDPE into the layers.
- The containers are believed to be the first of their kind and are recyclable. Incorporating recycled HDPE is much more complex than using polyethylene (PET).
- Last fall, P&G announced the development of a Spic & Span bottle made from 100 percent postconsumer recycled PET.

■ P&G uses over 100 million pounds of HDPE annually in its plastic bottles. Its goal is to develop a system that can use HDPE from any source, including P&G's own detergent bottles.

IMPLICATIONS: The concern displayed by P&G over the environment will probably spur consumers to purchase these products. Indeed, with competitive products being so similar in composition, companies will need to resort to extraordinary ways of creating uniqueness. Social and environmental issues will probably dictate the marketability of products in the near future.

REFERENCES: 1. "Procter & Gamble Unveils Recyclable Plastic Packaging," *Supermarket News,* May 1, 1989, p. 52.
              2. "How P&G Does It," *Chemical Marketing Reporter,* April 24, 1989, pp. 7, 21.

KEY WORDS: P&G, Downy, Liquid Tide, Liquid Cheer, Polyethylene

CHEMICAL/DETERGENT INDUSTRIES

Texaco Chemical Company has taken a major step toward its stated objective of becoming a broad-based supplier in the $3.5 billion U.S. laundry detergent market.

■ Under a joint agreement just signed with Ethyl Corporation, Texaco will take linear alcohols from Ethyl's Houston facility, ethoxylate them, and market the products under its established Surfonic trade name.

■ Nonylphenol ethoxylates, a market in which the company is fully integrated and in which it has a $50-million-plus market share, have been relegated largely to industrial applications and are not a major thrust in that market area.

■ In addition, the company's impact on the total surfactant business is obscured by the fact that its significant ethoxylation operation is seldom publicized.

■ Texaco's total ethoxylation capacity is rated at 200 million to 250 million pounds annually, making the company second only to Shell Chemical Company.

■ Texaco will offer eight different products based on three alcohols. The products will be 1- to 10-mole ethoxylates, with the largest volume expected to be in the 3- to 6-mole range.

- Alcohol ethoxylates, used directly as nonionic surfactants in laundry products, generally contain 6 to 12 moles of ethylene oxide (EO) per mole of alcohol; those used for production of alcohol ether sulfates contain 1 to 3 moles of EO.
- U.S. demand for alcohol ethoxylates is estimated to have been about 400 million pounds last year, with another 400-million-pound requirement for the ether sulfates, out of a total 4-billion-pound surfactant market.

IMPLICATIONS: The inevitable reduction of phosphorus use in detergents will create the need for replacement chemicals. It is possible that this void will be filled with ethylene-based materials, thus increasing the market share for this product. Texaco's increased production of alcohol ethoxylates will provide tremendous profits in the near future.

REFERENCES: 1. "Texaco Recasts Its Role in Big U.S. Detergents Mart," *Chemical Marketing Reporter,* June 5, 1989, pp. 3, 23.
2. "Ethyl and Texaco in Surfactants Deal," *Chemical Marketing Reporter,* May 29, 1989, p. 4.

KEY WORDS: Texaco, Shell, Alcohol Ethoxylates, Surfactants, Ethyl

Appendix E

Product Development

FINANCIAL SERVICES INDUSTRY

Many Pennsylvania banks are targeting mature individuals with retirement center branch locations. According to Ezekiel Ketchum, CEO of Meridian Bank, retirement center branches are shifting in branching strategy from a mass market approach to an effort to target specific market segments.

- The $9.7 billion bank, based in Reading, Pennsylvania, has opened an office at the Highlands, a retirement community in an upscale suburb of Reading.
- Generally, retirement center branches are staffed by two individuals and operated on limited hours, often opening four hours per day, three days per week. Employees are typically mature, sensitive, and empathetic individuals, according to Kathryn Donahue, a senior vice-president at First Fidelity. She also stated that residents expect service and can be demanding.
- The draw for banks in opening retirement center locations is that older people generally have money. According to Robert Stevens, president of Bryn Mawr Bank, the branches are a "nice, solid, traditional deposit business for banks." Bryn Mawr, a $280 million bank based in Pennsylvania, has two retirement center locations. The bank is planning to open a third branch in a new retirement center that was opened by the Marriott Corporation near its headquarters in Bethesda, Maryland.
- Retirement center locations are so desirable that First Fidelity, the superregional based in Newark, New Jersey, prepared a forty-page prospectus and a fifty-page operating manual, complete with testimonials, in attempting to beat out the competition for a retirement location.
- Several banks often vie for the right to open branches at any one retirement center.

REFERENCES: 1. "Philadelphia Banks Tap Older Market," *American Banker,* June 15, 1989, p. 10.
              2. "Senior Programs: Marketing Efforts Up," *Bank Advertising News,* July 3, 1989, pp. 3, 8.

KEY WORDS: Retirement Center Branches

Appendix F

Merger and Acquisition Activity

FINANCIAL SERVICES INDUSTRY

Security Pacific has agreed to sell a 5 percent stake in its nonbanking operations to Mitsui Bank of Japan in a deal worth $100 million. The transaction puts the value of SecPac's consumer and commercial services operations at fifteen times operating earnings. This is a high premium considering that SecPac's stock is trading at just seven times 1988 earnings on the New York Stock Exchange.

- Mitsui is Japan's seventh-largest bank with assets of $210 billion. The transaction will give the bank a stake in SecPac's international insurance, consumer and commercial finance, leasing, and other nonbanking operations, which contributed a combined $153 million to SecPac's bottom line last year. This equals a 1.2 percent return on the operation's $12.6 billion asset base. Mitsui has the right to purchase an additional 5 percent of these operations at the same price.

- SecPac and Mitsui are also partners in a commercial financing unit located in Japan. Security Pacific's CEO, Richard Flamson, and Mitsui's CEO, Kenichi Kamiya, have a close personal friendship.

- The sale was made in an effort to increase the value of SecPac's stock, which is trading at a multiple far below that of the market average. The market has valued the stock of major banks at a low multiple because of several problems, including the S&L crisis, the less-developed country debt situation, and the uncertain regulatory environment. Several of the most profitable and healthy banks, including SecPac and Fleet, have been negatively affected by market perceptions.

- Therefore, deals such as the SecPac-Mitsui joint venture are expected to become a standard for regional banks that have strong balance sheets and are seeking to increase their market value.

241

REFERENCES: 1. "Security Pacific to Sell Stakes to Mitsui Bank," *The Wall Street Journal*, June 14, 1989, p. A2.
               2. "Mitsui Bank to Buy Stake in Security Pacific Unit," *American Banker*, June 14, 1989, pp. 3, 23.

KEY WORDS: Security Pacific, Mitsui

AUTOMOTIVE/CAR RENTAL INDUSTRIES

Chrysler announced that it will acquire Thrifty Rent-A-Car System for $263 million. The deal is significant because it would make Chrysler the last of the Big 3 to take a stake in a major rental agency. Thrifty, based in Tulsa, Oklahoma, buys about 40,000 cars a year from Chrysler.

- On the average, Chrysler cars represent 75 percent to 80 percent of Thrifty's fleet. Clearly, however, this percentage will increase.
- The cash tender offer comes to about $27.75 per share for all of Thrifty's stock.
- Because GM and Ford hold large shares in the Big 4 rental car agencies (Hertz, Avis, Budget, and National), Chrysler was in danger of being edged out of the daily car rental market, which buys 10 percent of the total U.S. car production annually.
- Thrifty reported $79.3 million in revenues and $9.1 million in net income for the fiscal year ended June 30, 1988.
- The agency has an estimated 5.3 percent market share in the United States and has 357 locations in the United States and 301 abroad.

IMPLICATIONS: Clearly, the purchase of Thrifty by Chrysler will solidify its relationship with the car rental agency and possibly increase fleet sales. These sales have become an increasingly important factor in overall automotive sales, considering the expected downturn in the market. In addition to fleet sales, Chrysler should expand awareness of the agency through promotional tie-ins with its product lineup.

REFERENCES: 1. "Chrysler to Buy Rent-A-Car Company," *Ward's Automotive Reports*, May 22, 1989, p. 165.
               2. "Thrifty Buy Is Chrysler's Rental Shield," *Automotive News*, May 22, 1989, pp. 1, 57.
               3. "Chrysler to Buy Car Rental Firm for $263 Million," *The Wall Street Journal*, May 19, 1989, p. C16.

4. "Chrysler Agrees to Pay $263 Mil. for Thrifty Rent-A-Car Purchase," *Investor's Daily*, May 19, 1989, p. 31.
5. "Chrysler to Buy Thrifty Car Rental," *USA Today*, May 19, 1989, p. B1.
6. "Chrysler to Buy Thrifty Rent-A-Car," *The New York Times*, May 19, 1989, pp. D1, D3.

KEY WORDS: Chrysler, Thrifty

Appendix G

International

AUTOMOTIVE INDUSTRY

Environmental concerns have moved to the center stage of EEC politics as the ministers continue to embrace tough emission standards for automobiles.

- The new standards can cut pollution from small cars by an estimated 70 percent.
- Under the ministerial decisions, emission standards equivalent to those in force in the United States since 1983 will apply in the EEC to cars with engines of under 1.4 liters as of July 1, 1992, for new models, and six months later for other new cars.
- The EEC is allowing governments to offer tax incentives for the low-pollution cars between now and the end of 1992.

REFERENCES: 1. "Pollution Curbs for Cars Are Set by EEC Ministers," *The Wall Street Journal*, June 12, 1989, p. A11.
2. "Europe Sets Tough Small-Car Pollution Curbs," *Investor's Daily*, June 12, 1989, p. 26.

KEY WORDS: EEC, Emissions

West Germany's auto industry continues to disprove pessimistic forecasts of declining revenue and flat earnings.

- Many analysts have recently taken a more favorable view of BMW, Volkswagen, Daimler-Benz, and even Porsche AG.
- Earnings declines for BMW, VW, and Porsche are viewed as an unavoidable consequence of the auto industry's cyclical nature.
- During the first four months of 1989, new auto registrations in West Germany jumped 7.4 percent to 1 million units, and were about 9 percent in Italy, Britain, and France.
- Recently, BMW reported that group sales surged 23 percent in the first four months of 1989, and that pretax profits rose 6.9 percent to DM 990 million ($500.9 million).

244

IMPLICATIONS: Although the long-term prospects for the West German auto manufacturers may look optimistic, the fact remains that the Japanese represent a competitive threat to these manufacturers, particularly in the EEC markets and the United States. These competitive dynamics should affect BMW the most as it continues to rebuff diversification. Daimler-Benz, a company that is more of a conglomerate, has a thriving aerospace business, so it should be less vulnerable. Although Porsche has addressed its problems and is now less dependent on the U.S. market, many say that the company's only chance of long-term survival may be to merge with another company. Currently, it appears as though Volkswagen is in the best position (on a global basis) of all the West German auto manufacturers.

REFERENCES: 1. "The West German Auto Makers' Pace in '89 Defies
                  Bears," The Wall Street Journal, June 12, 1989, p. 9C.
               2. "Mercedes, BMW Stepping Up Competition in Home
                  Market," Investor's Daily, June 22, 1989, p. 29.

KEY WORDS: Volkswagen, Porsche, Daimler-Benz, BMW

CHEMICAL/DETERGENT INDUSTRIES

As of January 1, 1989, Henkel discontinued its production of phosphate-built detergents in West Germany. For the past fifteen years Henkel has been working on finding phosphate substitutes, and as early as 1983 the company had introduced phosphate-free detergents in Germany and Switzerland.

- Switzerland has banned usage of phosphates in detergents completely, and phosphate-built products now account for about 10 percent of the West German market.
- Between 1975 and 1985, use of phosphates in detergents fell from 276,000 tons to 160,000 tons in West Germany, and by 1987 it amounted to only 80,000 tons.
- Henkel has also replaced PVC bottles with polyethylene bottles for its liquid detergents and cleaners in response to public concern over dioxin emission during incineration of PVC bottles.
- Other innovations in this area include using a 5-liter carton lined with a thin plastic skin that, when empty, can be folded and the carton treated like any other paper waste.

IMPLICATIONS: Other manufacturers would be wise to discontinue phosphate-built detergents abroad as well as domestically. Now more than ever, environmental concerns are beginning to affect producers and product sales.

REFERENCES: 1. "Henkel Halts STPP Detergent Production in Germany," *Chemical Marketing Reporter,* May 15, 1989, p. 23.
2. "Henkel Moves to P-Free Detergents," *HAPPI,* June 1989, p. 24.

KEY WORDS: Henkel, Phosphate, West Germany, Switzerland, PVC Bottles

COSMETICS INDUSTRY

The U.S. import restrictions on Japanese cosmetics would jeopardize efforts at establishing U.S.-Japanese cooperation, the Cosmetic, Toiletry and Fragrance Association (CTFA) said at a U.S. Trade Representative (USTR) hearing on May 24.

- The USTR, after determining that Japan had committed unfair trade practices in the telecommunications trade, drafted a list of candidates for increased duties or import restrictions. The list includes beauty or makeup preparations, skin care, and sun care products.
- Japan is the U.S. cosmetic industry's third-largest foreign market. Exports to Japan increased 86 percent from 1986 to 1988, and imports from Japan rose 98 percent in the two-year period.
- The trade association noted that U.S. 1988 cosmetics sales in Japan were $877 million, representing 9.6 percent of the $9.2 billion total cosmetics sales in Japan.
- Max Factor sales in Japan reached $300 million in 1988; Avon totaled $224 million; Estée Lauder volume was $171 million; Revlon reached $79 million; Helene Curtis totaled $52 million; and Bristol-Myers realized $51 million.
- In addition, increased trade restrictions would harm U.S. companies that import Japanese ingredients and components. About $9 million worth of Japanese ingredients were imported in 1988.

IMPLICATIONS: If trade restrictions are increased, retaliation can be expected. Japanese firms and consumers will probably boycott U.S. cosmetics. The unfair telecommunications trade practices conducted by the Japanese do not affect the cosmetics industry. It is difficult to understand, then, how this action can do anything but cause further damage in an already difficult situation.

REFERENCES: 1. "U.S. 'Retaliatory' Import Restrictions on Japanese Cosmetics," *FDC Reports Rose Sheet,* May 29, 1989, p. 2.
               2. "Cosmetics May Suffer in Trade War," *Chemical Marketing Reporter,* May 29, 1989, pp. 7, 16.

KEY WORDS: CTFA, USTR, Max Factor, Avon, Estée Lauder, Revlon, Helene Curtis, Bristol-Myers

Appendix H

Sample Intelligence Newsletter

Environmental Facts: ISDN users are moving from trials to implementation. More and more applications are beginning to emerge. (*Electronics Journal* 4/13/89 p. 10C)

Competitive Activity: Four competing vendors have introduced similar products, and the major modem manufacturers are now targeting the terminal adapter market. (*Bits & Bytes* 3/89 p.46)

New Product Activity: Market research studies report that the life cycles for ISDN products will fall because product standards have not been established. Thus, product flexibility is the key. (*Electronics Today* 2/89 p. 10)

Pricing Activity: Prices for ISDN boxes are forecast to fall next year. Over the next five years, price competition will be intense as large OEMs enter the market. (*Telecom Week* 3/21/89 p. 66)

International Activity: Japanese and German vendors are almost certain to enter the ISDN market in the next two years. At the same time, U.S. companies may find it difficult to market in Germany and Japan. (*ISDN News*, 2/89 p. 101)

Appendix I

Sample Daily Intelligence Newsletter

DAILY BRIEFING: July 4, 1989

Good day. The major events of this Tuesday are:

MARKETS

- The DOLLAR rose slightly as traders reacted favorably to the recently published deficit figures.
- The STOCK MARKET rallied as the Dow increased 10 points to the 2,084 level, largely owing to the strength of the positive retail sales report after the Christmas season.
- Short-term INTEREST RATES have increased slightly as investors fear that the Fed will impose a tighter monetary policy.

RETAIL SALES

- The Commerce Department reported a sharp 0.9 percent increase in January, on the strength of higher auto and department store sales. Because of these encouraging figures and a low unemployment rate, the Fed should continue to keep a tight rein on the money supply. (NYT)

INSIDER TRADING

- The junk-bond chief of XYZ Investment Corporation is expected to be indicted soon. The company's recently announced settlement with prosecutors may negatively affect his defense. (WP p. A1)

PERSONNEL

- Dick Johnson, chairman of ABC Bank, purchased 100,000 shares for $2.5 million. The purchase, which was applauded by industry observers, was done to show confidence in his company. (NYT p. D1)

"TIDBITS"

- Keystone Bank may divest its discount brokerage service. (AB p. 3)
- The two major credit card vendors have implemented their own car rental insurance plans. (AB p. 1)
- The Big 3 automakers posted impressive output gains during 1988, compared with year-earlier levels. (LAT p. B7)

TOMORROW, THE TRADE DEFICIT AND CAPACITY UTILIZATION FIGURES ARE IN. THE TRADE FIGURES ARE OF PARTICULAR INTEREST TO THE INVESTMENT COMMUNITY BECAUSE THEY WILL AFFECT THE INTEREST RATE MARKET.

Appendix J

Detailed Questionnaire for Strategic Information Audit

Date of Interview: _____

Department: _____

Interviewee: _____

Interviewer: _____

INFORMATION SOURCES

1. What information sources do you use to obtain market intelligence or competitor intelligence?
2. How satisfied are you with these information sources as they pertain to your job function?
3. What is your budget on information sources?
4. What publications do you subscribe to? What is the total cost of subscriptions?
5. What publications that you do not receive should be acquired?
6. What elements would make your current information sources more valuable (for example, more timely information)?

INFORMATION DISTRIBUTION

7. In addition to your own department, to what other departments do you distribute information?
8. How frequently do you circulate information to other departments?
9. What information sources gathered by your group would be appropriate to put into a shared information network?

CRITICAL INFORMATION ISSUES

10. What type of information would you look for on a systematic or routine basis?
11. How would you like to see information indexed (by competitor, line of business, markets of interest)?
12. What emerging technologies, competitors, or businesses might threaten the market position of your group or even cause your group to be divested?

TIME FACTORS, EXPECTATIONS, AND FORMAT

13. How often would you like to see the information updated (daily, weekly, monthly, quarterly)?
14. What are your initial expectations of a business intelligence network? How will it benefit your role in the organization and your line of business?
15. In what format would you like to see the data of a business intelligence network? Would you rather have summarized abstracts, abstracts with analysis, or full text of a document?
16. How would you like to access this information (hard copy or floppy disk)?

OTHER

17. What are the future needs of a business intelligence network (for example, should it focus on regional markets, opportunities overseas, more competitive policies rather than actual products/services)?
18. What other marketing services would benefit your department and job function (for instance, qualitative research)?
19. Who else would you recommend we interview?
20. Which consulting firms have you hired over the past few years? What services have they performed and what did each firm charge?

Appendix K

Sample Monthly Intelligence Newsletter

Frozen Foods Division
Competitive Intelligence Highlights
March 1989

GREEN VEGETABLES

- According to an article in *Frozen Foods Digest,* Northland Corporation has introduced a new frozen okra that comes in a microwaveable container. Distribution is nationwide. An 8-ounce package retails for $1.59.
- Bob Gurney, our senior sales representative for the Southeast region, maintains that our major competitor is having problems distributing its products in Atlanta because of a trucking union dispute. For more information, contact Bob at (404) 555-1483.
- Arthur Siemens, one of our food scientists based at the R&D center, reported that he found a wealth of competitive information, including R&D expenditures, newly developing technologies, and food science applications, at the R&D Exposition in Chicago.
- Fresh Vegee, Inc. has unveiled a new line of frozen vegetables in the Pacific Northwest area of the United States. The line is premium priced.

Detailed information on these and other topics is available on the corporate intelligence network. For more information, contact Joseph Lugo, central coordinator, at extension 5990.

Appendix L

Worksheet for Developing a Shared Information Network

1. IDENTIFY Internal Champion

Choose an internal champion and department responsible for the network.

- Corporate/division marketing
- Information systems
- Strategic planning
- Marketing research
- Corporate library
- Newly created departments

2. ORGANIZE the Internal Effort

Organize maintenance/administrative duties and define the information management roles of those involved in the network.

- Procurement of data sources (working with outside suppliers and internal suppliers of information)
- Maintenance of the data base
- Feedback process
- End-user training
- Future growth/enhancements to the shared information network

Promote the system.

- "Selling" the system to top management
- Highlight benefits
- Set up demonstrations

3. DEVELOP a Work Plan

Develop a conceptual time frame for the network that is based around the immediate and long-term objectives of the organization.

- Evaluate end-user needs
- Analysis of needs
- Design of the prototype
- End-user feedback of the prototype
- Implementation of the system

4. BEGIN the Planning Phase

Identify long- and short-term goals for the system.

- Role of the network as a decision support system
- Avoiding potential pitfalls of the system
- Allowing for periodic evaluation and end-user feedback of the system

5. CONDUCT Strategic Information Audit

Conduct a survey that evaluates information needs and usages and identifies information "gaps" or duplication of effort.

- Survey design
- Conducting personal interviews
- Development of a blueprint that tracks the information flow of the organization
- Identify untapped information sources (for example, field intelligence)
- Evaluate investment in internal and external information sources

6. DEVELOP a Prototype

Develop a small-scale system that gives the users something to whet their appetites.

- Select initial content of the system from a wide variety of relevant information sources
- Integrate internal and external information
- Include bibliographic information of purchased studies
- Include a synthesis of the external literature
- Develop a user-friendly prototype that is key-word searchable

7. OBTAIN User Feedback

Obtain feedback for the purpose of making modifications to the system (format, data base design, and so on).

- Develop feedback survey
- Assure that the mix of information sources is optimal

- Allow for value-added elements to the information (for example, impact and implications)

8. DEVELOP the System

Amendments from initial prototype and investments in widespread distribution methods are made.

- Acquisition of hardware, software, communications equipment
- Task force trains select users for the system (systems coordinator)

9. ROLL OUT the System

Gradually increase the number of users of the network and "sell" the system to communicate the benefits.

- Presentations to senior management
- A corporate newsletter that highlights the system
- A minidemonstration or marketing scheme that is accessed via a personal computer or floppy disk
- Demonstrations at company conferences

10. ESTABLISH a Support Structure for the System

Develop a help or service function that is built into the system.

- Designed to resolve content issues, technical questions, and possible modifications
- May involve the creation of a separate job function or department responsible for providing users with system support
- Develop a hot line users can telephone for technical and information content support

11. PROMOTE Evolution of the System

Develop an organizational infrastructure to the network that evolves with the business to avoid the potential pitfalls of the network.

- Obtain a reasonable job commitment from the internal champion and the task force
- Secure a budget from top management
- Develop guidelines related to the security of the network
- Avoid pitfalls
- Internal "green-eyed monsters"
- The "not invented here" syndrome

Index

abstracts, from external sources, 225–247
acceptance, of shared information network, 72
accountability, security and, 75–76
accounting, and international information audit, 166
acquisitions, 42
  abstracts on, 241–243
advertisements, as information source, 119–120
analytical reports, 14, 101, 102–103
annual reports, 120, 180
architecture, system, 29–30, 35
archived information, 34, 78, 136
  value of, 104
artificial intelligence, 22, 33, 185, 191
assets, information as, 79
AT&T shared information network, 76
automation market research, 64–66
automotive industry, 123–124
  abstracts for, 226, 227, 231, 235–236, 242–243, 244–245
awards to employees, for information gathering, 146

awareness, corporate, of shared information network, 16–17, 48

barriers of communication, 21
BASIS software, 183
big business, strategic intelligence network in, 22–23
blueprint, for strategic intelligence, 90–94
books, 120
bottom line, 3, 199–210
  shared information network and, 47, 137
  strategic plan and, 5
bottom–up approach
  to strategic information audit, 84–85
  for system implementation, 197
brands, global identification of, 163
budget, for shared information network development, 72
business approach, 212–213

car rental industry, abstracts for, 242–243
cataloging system, 202
  ongoing maintenance of, 109
CD-ROM (compact disc-read only memory) technology, 136

257